AF425060

Genesis

Lyra Elowen

Published in the United States by Moonveil Siren Press

First Edition

Cover design and interior design by ChatGPT and Julie Mitchell
Printed in the United States of America

This novel was written by Lyra Elowen. Certain design elements and writing assistance were provided by AI (ChatGPT), but all creative authorship and copyright remain solely with Lyra Elowen.

This is a work of fiction. Names, characters, places, and incidents are either the product of the author's imagination or used fictitiously. Any resemblance to actual events or persons, living or dead, is entirely coincidental.

Dedication

For the ones who came before,
who wrote the impossible into truth,
and the truth into prophecy.

*To **Octavia E. Butler**,*
who gave us the language of resistance in futures bent on erasure.
To the storytellers of Black speculative fiction,
who made survival a sacred art.

*To comic book writers including **Stan Lee** and **Jack Kirby**,*
*and to **Garth Ennis** and **Darick Robertson**,*
for revealing power, mutation, and monstrosity as reflections of the
same truth.

To the minds who saw the world differently,
who were told their way of thinking was broken
when it was simply ungovernable.
You showed me how to see Lucien.
You helped me see myself.

To those erased in real time,
whose names never reached the page,
but whose lives are written into every system this story condemns.

This story is for every writer, artist, and rebel
who dared to imagine survival,
not as an end,
but as a revolution.

—L.E., J.M.

I

Dr. Lucien Tenebris sat rigid on the edge of his armchair, fingernails bitten raw, a thin sheen of sweat glistening across his temples. The television flickered, playing the same footage he'd watched a hundred times before. Damn near three years ago.

November 2028.

The day Malrick Vaughn was chosen president-elect—and shot.

The gunshot echoed still, sharp in his ears, though the world outside his home was quiet. The crowd's panic, captured in grainy pixels, pressed into him like a weight. He could almost feel the heat of the bodies around the stretcher, the smell of blood and fear.

Three days.
Three days the world held its breath.
Three days of relentless news, of faces frozen in horror, of hashtags, protests, and conspiracy threads blurring together in a fog of panic.

Then, on the third day, at 9:42 a.m., the announcement came.

Dead. Gone. Heart shattered. Nothing.

Lucien's hand shook as he pressed the remote into the cushion beside him. He could hear the echo of his own heartbeat, thundering against his ribs. He stayed. He couldn't leave. Couldn't turn away.

Then... the impossible.

At 12:12 p.m., under the sheet, Vaughn moved. A twitch. A grimace. Fingers curling, reaching for the ticket pinned to his toe. Doctors froze, the color draining from their faces. Lucien's stomach turned; nausea clawed up from his gut. His leg bounced faster, a metronome of panic.

Something in the room shifted. The air felt wrong, heavy, the walls themselves holding their breath. His pulse hammered, a drumbeat echoing the impossible truth: the world had not ended, yet everything had.

Dr. Yusra Khoury gently placed her hand on Lucien's bouncing knee, stilling it.

"It's over."

Lucien shook his head.

"It was only the beginning."

Yusra's eyes sank to the floor, a pit opening in her stomach as dread settled in. She looked up at him.

"Revelation 13, chapters 3 through 5."

Lucien's eyes darted to her hair, avoiding eye contact.

"You lost me with your biblical lore. What are you talking about?"

"One of the heads of the beast seemed to have been fatally wounded, but the wound healed. The whole world was amazed and followed the beast. People worshiped the dragon, Satan, because he gave authority to the beast. They worshiped the beast too, saying, 'Who is like the beast? Who can fight against it?' The beast was allowed to speak great blasphemies against God and to control and intimidate the people for forty-two months."

"That must be the most absurd horse shit I've ever heard."

"That passage describes the anti-Christ."

Lucien laughed, but it was hollow. His hands chipped at his fingernails.

"The anti-Christ? You think Vaughn is the anti-Christ?"

"You don't?" Yusra asked, her tone steady, almost dangerous in its calm.

"I think it's utter nonsense," he said, his voice tight.

Her eyes lingered on him, unblinking. "If you think it's nonsense now... wait until the world catches up."

A crackle from the television was heard beneath their conversation. A television broadcast, celebrating the man who tasted and survived death, the man who increasingly made life more difficult for those under his reign. Televangelist Pastor Nash's voice echoed against the walls of Lucien's living room.

"As it is proclaimed in Luke 24:46, ' Thus it is written, and thus it behoved Christ to suffer, and to rise from the dead the third day.' Folks, President Vaughn is not a stingy politician. He is the second coming of Christ! This is our Messiah! God so pleased it that Jesus returned to us in the form of a just, righteous, and powerful ruler! Praise be to God! Praise be to Christ! Praise be to Malrick Vaughn!"

Yusra scoffed at the sermon. "Malrick Vaughn may very well be the furthest thing from a second coming of Christ."

November 2028.

Malrick Vaughn adjusted his tie in the full-length mirror, eyes sharp, posture perfect. There was a soft knock at the door.

"You don't have to be so polite, Samuel. Just come in."

A man entered, clad in black from head to toe. No hesitation. No emotion. A pistol appeared in his hand, pressed to the back of Vaughn's head. Vaughn turned slowly, calm, unflinching.

"No need for theatrics, Samuel," he said, his voice smooth, almost casual.

Samuel's fingers tightened around the pistol. Vaughn pulled a wad of bills from his jacket pocket, counting deliberately. "Your shot was damn near perfect."

Samuel snatched the money, scanning each bill, making sure every promised dollar was accounted for. Vaughn's eyes never left him, calculating, measuring, as if weighing a future the world hadn't yet dared to see.

For a heartbeat, silence fell heavily on the room. Then, Samuel nodded, satisfied. The pistol lowered. Vaughn's grin was faint, subtle, a predator acknowledging the competence of another predator.

He thought briefly, almost silently: Perfect. Just as it must be.

The calm precision, the audacity, the control. Lucien would later call it impossible, unnatural. At that moment, however, Vaughn was simply... him. The world had not yet begun to understand what was coming.

II

Lucien Tenebris preferred mornings before the sun had decided what temperature the world should be. The quiet of the morning always helped his shoulders ease. No chattering outside the window. No headlights of cars passing by. Just quiet.

The half-light poured into the narrow kitchen of his small house in a muted wash of gray-blue, soft enough not to startle him. His home was quiet, the kind of quiet he curated with intention. No ticking clocks. No humming appliances left on overnight. Only the low creak of settling wood and the familiar rhythm of his own movements. Mercury approached him, his full, gray coat brushing against his pajama pant leg as he approached his food dish. His cat was one of the few that could touch him without startling him or driving him into a mental frenzy. Mercury enjoyed a quiet morning in solitude almost as much as Lucien.

The kettle whistled too sharply. He flinched and switched it off before it reached its full shrill. Tea. He should drink tea. People insisted it helped. He brewed it wrong, as always, too much heat, leaves sitting far too long. It tasted like burnt soil. He drank it anyway, standing alone at the counter because sitting felt too slow this early.

He dressed quickly, choosing clothes by texture rather than aesthetics: soft cotton, worn sleeves, dark colors that didn't shout at him visually. He tugged the collar flat three times until the seams aligned properly on his shoulders.

Before leaving, he paused at the threshold. His front door had a groove worn into the frame, a tiny notch he pressed his finger into every morning. He didn't know when the habit began. It anchored him, so he touched it. One slow press. One silent breath.

He stepped outside. The air was cold and honest. His house sat on a quiet street near the edge of campus, close enough to walk but far enough from the dorms that the nights were still. He liked the space. The distance. The illusion of control over how much of the world reached him. He inhaled and exhaled, watching the fog of the crisp morning leave his lips, mentally preparing himself. The peaceful quiet of the morning wouldn't last, and he knew it.

The walk to the university cut through a small residential stretch before opening into the quad. Students were already gathering, their morning chatter rising in chaotic bursts that prickled against his ear drum. Lucien adjusted his scarf and shoved his hands in his coat pockets, moving along the outer path, skirting the crowds, keeping his body angled to avoid any chance of someone brushing too close.

He didn't like touch. Touch was too loud.

Whitfield Hall appeared ahead, the oldest building on campus, always smelling faintly of bleach and oxidized metal. He slipped inside. The fluorescent lights buzzed in mismatched rhythms and pitches overhead. His jaw clenched. His fingers drifted to the seam of his sleeve, tracing it compulsively, grounding himself in the small repetition.

Someone turned the corner too quickly. A student. Carrying too many books. Not watching where he was going. They collided. Skin met skin. The student's fingertips brushed the inside of Lucien's wrist for less than a second, but enough.

Lucien inhaled sharply, eyes going wide. The jolt hit him like a flashbulb behind his eyelids. Not sight, not sound. A fragment:

A stovetop burner left on.
The smell of burnt eggs.
A harsh voice shouting, "Hurry up, we're late—"
A bathroom stall door slamming.
A woman's sinking thought, I can't do another day of this.

Lucien stumbled back, one hand hitting the wall. The student blinked, startled. "Dr. Tenebris, I'm so sorry—I didn't see—"

"Watch it," Lucien rasped, too sharp, too fast. Then softer, almost strangled:

"...It's fine. Just—go."

The student apologized again and hurried away. Lucien stayed pressed to the wall until his breathing leveled into something functional, the metronome inside his head syncing with his breath. He was lucky he was forced to take piano lessons throughout his younger years; otherwise, his grounding technique would be greatly flawed. He scrubbed at his wrist as if he could erase the echo clinging there, the taste of someone else's panic still metallic at the back of his tongue.

Not now. Not today.

He closed his eyes and exhaled through his nose, forcing the fragment back into the mental corner where he buried all the others. Sensory overload. Migraine aura. Stress. He'd told himself every explanation except the real one.

He reached his classroom early, as always. The board was a welcome surface, something simple he could control. He wrote clean, precise formulas until the students filled the room in a rising tide of noise. He tolerated it. Barely.

His lecture was crisp, brilliant, and emotionally distant. Alchemy made sense to him in ways people didn't. He found refuge in dissolution, distillation, transformation, concepts that required no eye contact, no small talk, no touch.

By the time class ended, he felt wrung out. He retreated to his office, shut the door, and let the quiet fold around him like a weighted blanket. He sat at his desk and opened his laptop. Emails loaded. He ignored the first seven.

Lucien was about to close his laptop when a bold subject line captured his attention.

"MANDATORY STAFF MEETING, 5PM, STUDENT CENTER, ROOM 37."

He rolls his eyes in disdain. His return to home, to his cat, would have to wait.

He enters room 37, a room intended for media events, sometimes used as a classroom for the large mandatory general education classes. He surveyed the room, noting an empty seat in the very back corner, no one sitting near it. His shoulders lax just a little, as he approaches the seat and sits so he can tune out the next 45 minutes of absolute nonsense which could have easily been an email.

Numerous members stand in front of the faculty, including the dean, some of his administrative assistants, and police officers. Nearly 10 minutes into the meeting, the door rams open. A Palestinian woman enters, scrambling to hold her stack of papers and books, donning a royal blue hijab. The administrator up front raises an eyebrow.

"Dr. Khoury, it would behoove you and the rest of us to arrive in a timely fashion,"

"I'm sorry, I'm sorry – I've only just started a week ago. Still haven't figured out the layout of this place."

The administrator continues, as Dr. Khoury sits right next to Lucien, her covered arm brushing against his. Lucien folds his arms close to him, attempting to shove himself as deep into the corner of the wall as possible to make sure he no longer has to touch her.

Another 10 minutes pass, then Dr. Khoury looks over at Lucien, her eyes traveling him in recognition. She whispers excitedly.

"Aren't you Dr. Tenebris?"

Lucien continues staring at the presentation, giving only a curt nod. That should be enough. It usually is, but Dr. Khoury inhales sharply, delighted.

"I thought it was you," she whispers. "I read your dissertation last year."

Lucien's eyes flick to her, quick and suspicious, as if she'd claimed to read his diary.

"My—why?" he mutters.

She beams. "It was fascinating. The parallels you drew between alchemical stages and neural restructuring? Brilliant. Utterly strange, but brilliant."

Lucien's face twitches, uncertain if he's being mocked. "Strange?"

"In the best way," she insists. "Academia needs strange."

He doesn't know what to do with that, so he turns back toward the projector. The administrator drones on about budget updates and campus safety protocols. Lucien debates, quietly, whether it would be socially acceptable to fake a heart attack and leave.

Yusra leans slightly toward him again, not enough to touch, but enough to exist at the edge of his peripheral vision.

"I'm still learning my way around," she whispers. "Every hallway looks the same to me. Do you teach here in this building?"

Lucien presses his lips into a flat line. Talking during these meetings feels like breaking a rule. Ignoring her feels harder.

"I teach in Whitfield Hall."

"Oh! The old chemistry building?"

"More like the old everything building," he mutters.

She smiles, a soft, patient smile that makes him feel inexplicably seen and extremely uncomfortable at the same time. Another fifteen minutes of speeches pass. Lucien stares at the wall just above the presenters' heads, willing the clock to accelerate by sheer hatred alone. At last, the dean closes his folder.

"Alright, everyone. Thank you for your time."

The moment the meeting ends, Lucien is the first person standing. His muscles coil with the need to escape the crowd before someone traps him in conversation. He shoves his laptop into his bag and pivots toward the door.

"Dr. Tenebris?"

He sighs internally and turns. Yusra has gathered her papers into a lopsided stack, clutching them against her chest. Her blue hijab frames her face like a calm flame.

"I didn't mean to bother you earlier," she says, adjusting her grip. "I really did enjoy your work."

Lucien shifts his weight, unsure whether to thank her or run.

She continues, "Actually, I meant to ask. Would you be free for a moment? There's a small bakery near here. It's the only place I've found that makes proper ka'ek with za'atar."

She hesitates, a flicker of vulnerability passing through her voice. "It reminds me of home."

Lucien blinks. He recognizes the faint tremor that comes with the word home. He hears it sometimes in himself, though never aloud.

"I was going anyway," she adds, gently. "If you'd like to join me. No pressure."

Lucien glances at the door. His cat. His quiet home. His safe routines. Then he glances back at her, this earnest stranger who somehow managed to sit next to him, brush against him, compliment him, confuse him, and not repel him all within forty-five minutes.

"...Are there people there?" he asks finally.

"Not usually," she says. "The owner bakes through the afternoon. It smells like sesame and warm bread. Peaceful." She softens. "You won't have to talk if you don't want to."

Lucien exhales through his nose, a near-silent, reluctant surrender.

"Fine," he mutters. "But only because the meeting was awful and I deserve something to eat."

Yusra's smile blooms. "Then ka'ek it is."

"You can call me Lucien, by the way."

She giggles. "Yusra."

She steps aside to let him walk ahead, respecting his space, without being told. For reasons he cannot articulate, Lucien finds himself slowing his pace so she can walk beside him instead.

The bakery was just at the corner near the university. It comforted Lucien to see one car in the small parking lot. At least if he wasn't going to follow routine, he wouldn't be interrupted by the continued noise of college-aged chatter ringing in his ears.

They step inside, the smell of warmth and comfort inviting him through the doorway, the bakery warmly lit. The man at the counter sees Yusra, offering her a hug and a small kiss on the cheek.

"Yusra! The usual today?"

"Actually, I'd like to buy a second for my friend, Lucien."

Lucien's eyebrows raise at the word. Friend?

The man at the counter only smiles, gesturing to Lucien. "Of course!" He claps his hands towards the kitchen. "Please, 2 ka'ek with za'atar!"

Yusra and Lucien quietly make their way to a table, the bakery empty at this hour.

They sit across from one another, the empty bakery humming softly with the sound of ovens cooling. For Lucien, it feels like a safe pocket of air: quiet, warm, no students, no fluorescent lights buzzing overhead. He doesn't know what to do with his hands, so he folds them over one another on the table, then refolds them when that feels wrong, then settles for gripping one wrist beneath the table. Yusra notices, but she doesn't comment. She sets her papers down beside her and exhales, tension leaving her shoulders.

"I'm sorry about earlier," she says softly. "The meeting. I didn't mean to whisper so much. I know it's... distracting."

Lucien shakes his head. "The meeting itself was distracting. You were... fine."

The compliment sounds rough, scraped out of gravel, but sincere.

Yusra smiles, biting back a small laugh. "I'll take that."

The baker arrives with two warm sesame rings wrapped in paper. He sets them down gently before returning to the kitchen, humming something in Arabic under his breath. The smell hits Lucien first: nutty, herbal, deeply grounding. Yusra closes her eyes for a breath, reverent, like she's touching a memory.

"This," she says quietly, "was always sold on street corners back home. After school, after work, after anything difficult. You'd walk past and the smell alone would fix half your problems."

She tears off a small corner, dips it in the za'atar folded inside, and waits for him to try his. Lucien hesitates only a moment before taking a bite. Warm. Chewy. Bright with spice. Comforting in an unfamiliar way.

His eyebrows lift. "This is... unexpectedly good."

Yusra beams. "You say strange things with such seriousness."

"I'm not joking," he insists. "Most food is either bland or too stimulating. This is balanced." He pauses. "Predictable, in a good way."

"That's the best review I've ever heard," she says, laughing softly into her hand.

They eat in companionable silence for a moment. Lucien keeps his eyes mostly on the table, or the food, or the window. Never quite on her, but never quite away either. Finally Yusra speaks again, quieter this time.

"I didn't mean to... well. I hope it wasn't inappropriate, what I said in the meeting." Her fingers trace the lip of her cup. "About your dissertation."

Lucien frowns slightly. "Why would it be inappropriate to say you liked something?"

"Because some people don't like being told they're brilliant," she says. "Some people think it's sarcasm or pity."

Lucien blinks, taken aback by the precision of her insight.

"My work isn't brilliant," he mutters. "It's niche. Odd."

"Niche doesn't mean lesser," she replies. "Odd doesn't mean

wrong. Some of the most important ideas begin as the strange ones."

Lucien shifts, uncomfortable. Praise feels like a spotlight he can't step out of.

Yusra softens. "I meant it genuinely. That's all."

His fingers twitch beneath the table. A small stim, quickly hidden.

Lucien clears his throat, eyes fixed on the table. "Your name is... unusual."

Yusra raises an eyebrow, amused. "Unusual?"

"Not in a bad way," he says quickly. "Just uncommon. Distinct. I haven't heard it before."

Her smile curls, soft and entertained.

"So that's your way of giving compliments?"

Lucien blinks, thrown. Compliment? He opens his mouth, closes it, then mutters, "I didn't mean it negatively."

"I know," she says gently. "And I accept it."

She tears another small piece of ka'ek, dipping it into the za'atar. Lucien watches her hands more than her face. It's easier that way.

Lucien finally looks up at her then, just a flicker, meeting her eyes before glancing away again. Something warm and uncomfortable sits in his chest, unfamiliar. She breaks the moment gently.

"So... alchemy," she says, tilting her head. "Do you think people misunderstand your field on purpose, or just out of habit?"

Lucien huffs. "Both. Mostly both."

"Yet you teach it."

"Someone has to," he mutters. "Otherwise the department chair will assign it to someone who thinks alchemy is just 'old chemistry' and not a philosophical discipline with symbolic structure, psychological parallels, cross-cultural significance—"

He cuts himself off when he realizes he's rambling. Yusra's smile is not mocking. It's warm. Interested. Encouraging.

"You care about it a great deal," she says softly.

Lucien swallows. "It makes sense to me."

"Then that's reason enough to teach it."

Her words land with a gentleness he isn't used to. He tries another bite of ka'ek. It gives him something to do, something predictable to anchor him.

"...Why theology?" he asks suddenly.

Yusra exhales, a soft, bittersweet sound. "Because stories shape people. Sometimes more than truth does. I wanted to understand why."

Lucien nods as if that answer is deeply, personally acceptable. She looks at him for a long moment, not pitying, not prying, observing the way he struggles to sit comfortably in his own skin.

"I'm glad you came with me," she says quietly.

Lucien's throat tightens, just a little. "The meeting was terrible," he repeats. "I needed something edible."

"Now you have it," she says, smiling. He doesn't realize he's smiling back, a small, reluctant, uneven thing, until she notices and her expression softens even further.

Outside, dusk pools violet across the pavement. Inside, warmth settles between them, a quiet agreement neither of them fully understands yet.

III

Ever since Vaughn rose from the dead, he began touring Sunday services, calling it his "Miracle Tour." Churches filled, lines wrapping around them, to witness the president at work.

In the weeks after his resurrection, a strange fever swept the country, not illness, but anticipation. Billboards lit up with REVIVED. ANOINTED. RETURNED. Megachurches requested him months in advance. Evangelical networks replayed the slowed footage of him awakening beneath a hospital sheet like it was scripture.

The first appearance was in Alabama. The second in Missouri. Then Georgia, Florida, the Carolinas, Texas. Word spread faster than government press releases could keep up. People camped overnight outside church doors. Families brought sick relatives wrapped in blankets, waiting for a touch. Children held cardboard signs reading, "HEAL ME."

By the third week, security officers had become ushers. By the fifth, the "Miracle Tour" had its own theme music.

Whenever Vaughn entered a sanctuary, the air shifted.
It tightened, humming through the rafters like a tuning fork

struck too hard. His eyes appeared too bright beneath the stage lights. His hands stayed bare, always bare, as he descended from the pulpit with the measured grace of a man entirely certain of his influence.

The first "healing" happened quietly. A woman with tremors stepped forward. Vaughn laid a palm against her cheek. She gasped, a sharp, broken sound, and collapsed, limbs rigid for a breath before going limp. The congregation erupted.

"She's healed!"
"Glory!"
"Look what God can do!"

Ushers swiftly carried her behind the pulpit. From the front row, it looked miraculous. From the side aisles, it looked rehearsed. From the choir loft, where the angle was wrong, it looked like her soul had been pulled through her skin.

The second "healing" hit harder. A teenage boy stepped forward. Vaughn touched his forehead. The boy seized. A sound tore from him, half sob, half swallowed scream, before his body sagged into Vaughn's waiting arms. He was dragged away by security. The choir didn't miss a beat.

Reporters wrote glowing exposés. Influencers cried on livestreams. Hashtags trended: #TheHandOfGod and #MiracleVaughn. Inside the sanctuaries, patterns emerged. Some people swooned. Some people fainted.

A rare few... hit Vaughn like electricity. Those were different. When he touched them, his pupils dilated instantly. His body trembled slightly, a tremor he hid behind practiced smiles. The flush along his throat deepened. He inhaled sharply, as though tasting something exquisite.

Always — always — those individuals were carried away fastest. No one asked where. The crowd was too busy praising. Sometimes it was a businessman in a suit. Sometimes a teenage girl in a denim jacket. Sometimes an elderly man gripping a cane. It didn't matter.

Once Vaughn's eyes widened, just a flicker, a glint, the guards closed in. Witnesses described it differently:

"It was healing."
"It was deliverance."
"It was rapture."

From the balconies, where the view was wider, it looked like a feeding.

When Vaughn touched the third congregant, a boy whose whole body jolted as though struck by lightning, the air in the sanctuary thickened. Vaughn staggered back a half-step, eyes blown wide for the briefest moment, pupils swallowing half the iris. The crowd erupted in praise.

"Hallelujah!"
"He's healed!"
"Praise be!"

Vaughn did not raise his hands again. He bowed his head. At least, that's what the congregation believed, that their resurrected president was humbling himself before God, whispering prayers of gratitude. They didn't see the truth. The small black earpiece tucked beneath the curl of his hair. The way his lips barely moved, not in prayer, but in instruction. A murmur, soft as a confession:

"Code white. A live one. Male. Approximately 8 years old. Rear exit."

To the cheering congregation, his posture was holy devotion. To the unseen operatives listening through the line, it was a directive. The boy's limp body was lifted swiftly, carried behind the curtain with carefully practiced efficiency. The choir swelled, drowning the moment in triumphant song.

No one noticed the mother in the third row whose scream was swallowed by the music as she reached for the space her son had occupied. No one noticed Vaughn's faint shiver of pleasure. No one noticed the phrase he whispered next:

"Send a retrieval van."

To the crowd, he was performing miracles. To Section 9, he was feeding them intel.

By month two, several families quietly reported missing relatives after attending services. Law enforcement dismissed their concerns as "confusion amid large gatherings." Meanwhile, Vaughn grew stronger. More charismatic. More radiant. More terrifyingly alive. His smile sharpened. His eyes gleamed too quickly. His voice grew smoother, richer, hypnotic. Whatever had pulled him back from death was thriving.

Then, as his administration soared forward, the tour expanded into the first year, the second year, the third year, in a packed sanctuary in Atlanta, as the choir's voices rose to a trembling crescendo, a woman stood in the back row, notebook pressed to her chest.

Dr. Yusra Khoury.

She had come seeking the truth. She came seeking research. The moment Vaughn touched the first trembling woman and her body folded like a puppet with its strings cut, Yusra's breath caught in her throat.

The congregation screamed miracle. Yusra saw something else entirely. She saw the truth.

IV

Another day of teaching left Lucien alone in his classroom, sitting at his desk as the fading chatter of students dissolved into silence. His eyes were glued to his laptop, hyper-focused on entering grades, a task he loathed with every fiber of his being. The keys clacked beneath his fingers, steady and rhythmic, until the softest footfalls crept into the room.

He didn't look up at first. Only when the presence loomed just close enough did he lift his gaze.

A figure stood before him, stark and chilling: black dress shoes, black suit, black gloves, and a smooth blank mask that swallowed all traces of humanity. A shiver broke up Lucien's spine.

The figure extended a yellow envelope stamped with a violent red CONFIDENTIAL. The voice that emerged from behind the mask was modulated, distorted, distant.

"Please review the proposal, Dr. Tenebris. A response is required within twenty-four hours."

Lucien opened his mouth, but nothing came out. The figure was already gone, footsteps fading with mechanical precision. He exhaled slowly, then peeled open the envelope. A stack of freshly printed forms slid into his hands.

GRANT OPPORTUNITY: ALCHEMICAL NEURAL SCIENTIST NEEDED

His breath stalled. The salary was exponentially higher than his university pay. The project involved analyzing neural chemistry in volunteers who had undergone extreme trauma, refining and isolating compounds. On paper, it was a perfect fit for him. Too perfect. Too strange. Why would a grant be delivered like a threat? Why the mask? Why the secrecy?

Why twenty-four hours?

His pulse ticked uncomfortably in his ears.

That was when Yusra stepped into the doorway, a chaotic stack of papers jutting from her satchel. She caught sight of him and smiled, a warm, grounding moment, and he returned the faintest corner-lift of a grin, eyes darting everywhere except her face.

"You ready for our afternoon ka'ek?" she asked, brushing hair from her cheek. "I need listening ears. A *lot* has happened this weekend."

He nodded. More eagerly than he intended. Outside of Mercury, she was the only person he genuinely enjoyed being around, a fact that still startled him whenever he thought about it.

The bakery greeted them with warmth and spice and the

comforting bustle of late afternoon chatter.

"Yusra and Lucien! My favorites!" the baker called. He swept Yusra into a hug, then offered Lucien a softer nod and smile. "Two ka'ek wit' za'atar, comin' right up!"

As they sat, Yusra landed heavily in her chair, exhaling sharply. Lucien caught it immediately, the tension radiating from her posture, the storm brewing behind her eyes.

"Something wrong?" he asked gently.

She pulled out her journal. "Have you heard of Vaughn's Miracle Tours?"

Lucien scoffed. "I wish I hadn't. How delusional must people be to cling to biblical nonsense so tightly they think Vaughn is connected to it?"

Yusra blinked, startled, not offended, but thrown.

"I... actually agree with you," she said. "Not about it being 'biblical nonsense,' as you so lovingly put it, but there's a twisted mutation that Americans keep making out of Scripture."

She flipped to yesterday's journal entry.

"People call him a savior, a healer, but there's no healing happening. People collapse. They convulse. He doesn't heal them. He... takes something. From them."

Lucien stilled. "Feeding off them?"

"I know it sounds bizarre, but his reactions, the dilated pupils, the salivation... I recognize those physical signs. Something dark is happening. Look."

She pulled out printouts: missing persons reports, hospital notes about unexplained comas.

"These aren't miracles. They're casualties, yet people are praising him."

Lucien's hands tightened around his ka'ek. He nodded, silent. Far too silent. Yusra noticed.

"What about you? Are you okay? Something's off."

The bold red CONFIDENTIAL flashed in his mind.

He swallowed hard. "Not here."

Her brow lifted. "Not... here?"

"There's a lot to explain. Can we talk at my home? It's close."

Her concern sharpened. She nodded without hesitation.

"Of course."

They left half their ka'ek behind. Lucien walked with stiff shoulders, hands buried deep in his pockets, eyes trained forward. Yusra kept pace, stealing glances. He looked afraid. Terrified.

At his door, a paper was pinned to the frame. Lucien lunged to snatch it before she could see, but not fast enough.

"What was that?" she asked softly.

"Nothing. I'll take care of it."

"Was that an eviction notice?"

"I said I'll take care of it."

She fell silent.

Inside, the air smelled faintly of burnt tea leaves, metallic and bitter. Lucien motioned for her to sit while he rifled through his bag. Mercury trotted in cautiously, then, sensing Yusra, approached like a magnet drawn to warmth. He brushed her leg, then curled into her lap as though he'd known her forever, meeting her lap with gentle purring.

Lucien glanced over and huffed a shy, breathy laugh.
"He... doesn't usually do that."

"What's his name?" she asked, voice warm.

"Mercury."

Yusra's face lit up. "Mercury? Lucien, that is so perfectly you."

Mercury pressed his paws deeper into the cushion, purring louder as if he agreed.

Lucien's shoulders eased. Something unspoken and gentle settled between them, the kind of warmth that only forms when a guarded person lets someone step one layer closer. Yusra softened instantly, stroking Mercury's head. Lucien finally produced the yellow envelope and handed it to her. She read carefully.

"A job opportunity?" she murmured. "Are you leaving the university?"

"I haven't decided," he said. "They gave me twenty-four hours."

She scanned the header again. Section 9.

"What is that? Some government branch?"

"I... assume so. The work matches my research perfectly."

"It does." She smiled sadly. "It honestly reads like someone used your dissertation as a blueprint."

Then she met his eyes.

"How do *you* feel? I can sense it. You're afraid. Why?"

He wrung his hands, raw skin rubbing raw skin.

"It was how it was delivered," he finally said. "A man in all black. Blank mask. Modulated voice. He walked in, handed it to me, walked out."

Yusra shuddered. "You had every right to be afraid."

Lucien exhaled toward the dining table where the eviction notice rested like a silent accusation.

"The money though..."

Yusra's face softened.

"You don't have to face this alone, Lucien. If you're weighing your options... you're right, the timing is suspicious; however, only your heart knows what's right."

He stared at his bruised palms.

"I want to work in a real lab. My own lab. Quiet. Alone. With focus. Teaching is... fine, but it's never felt like mine. The requirement to adhere to forced standards, the constant drifting of apathetic young minds. I want to enjoy science again."

"Then there's your answer," she said gently.

Her eyes drifted to the eviction notice.

"In the meantime... I have a suggestion. I've been living in a hotel for months. It seems you've been overwhelmed trying to juggle everything. Let me help. You have a spare bedroom. I can move in, split the mortgage, just until you're stable again."

He sank back, ashamed. "I can't ask you to uproot your life for me."

"You're not asking." She smiled. "I'm offering. Would that feel safe for you? I know you and Mercury love your peace. I promise I'll protect it."

Mercury flexed his claws into the cushion and purred louder, as if endorsing the decision.

Lucien let out a thin, surprised laugh.

"I don't think Mercury will let me say no."

Yusra laughed softly with him. Just like that, it was decided.

Their friendship shifted into something steadier, deeper. Two lives braided together out of necessity, trust, and the fragile hope that this was the beginning of something good.

Something stable. Something safe. Even though neither of them had any idea how wrong they were.

V

The satisfaction of wiping formulas from the board one last time brought a rare ease to Lucien's shoulders. He was an avid believer that a clear space made a clear mind. For once, the clutter of anxiety stepped back and gave him room to breathe.

Accepting the job had been stranger than the offer itself. The confidential documents included just one final instruction:

"TO ACCEPT, PLEASE CALL 999-9999."

It was absurd. It was 2031. Who still required phone calls? He muttered to himself as he dialed,

"It is two-thousand thirty-one. Why am I picking up a phone when the internet exists?"

The line clicked before he could speak. A modulated voice answered:

"Lucien Tenebris. Status: accepted. Report to onboarding in exactly two weeks."

The line immediately went dead. Lucien stared at his phone, stunned. What kind of work demanded that level of secrecy? That impersonality?

He pushed the thought down. For every detail that unsettled him about Section 9, its rewards came back tenfold. A real lab. Real funding. A chance to work directly with neural chemistry instead of fighting through endless stacks of essays.

He packed the last of his notes into the cardboard box when Yusra entered the room. She stopped in the doorway, eyes widening at the emptiness of his once chaotic classroom.

"I can't believe it..." she breathed. "You're really going."

Lucien offered a shy, awkward smile.

"I am."

Relief washed over her face.

"At least we'll still have Mercury and ka'ek at night."

A real smile, rare and warm, tugged across Lucien's features. Yusra had long ago taken over their evening tea; her warm sesame-scented ka'ek had officially replaced the stink of every burnt batch he had ever produced. He wasn't even trusted near the kettle anymore.

She nodded toward the door.

"I was about to head home. Want to walk together?"

He nodded and lifted the box. They stepped out of Whitfield Hall together for the last time. The university grounds greeted them with hostility. The moment they crossed the threshold, a group of students spotted Yusra and began shouting:

"Get out of here, terrorist!"
"Jesus hates you!"
"Abomination!"
"You should be ashamed!"

Something hard clattered against Yusra's shoulder. Another object hit her arm. She flinched, trying to shield her face as she slowly crumpled toward the ground. Lucien froze for half a heartbeat, then lunged, kneeling beside her and lifting the box as a shield against the barrage. Laughter hissed through the air. The students scattered. Silence settled in the aftermath, sharp and ugly.

Lucien could feel the devastation radiating from her, but her expression remained almost entirely composed save for a slight shine in her eyes. She brushed off her sleeves and whispered:

"Please... let's just get home."

He nodded quickly. They hurried the rest of the way, and once inside, Lucien locked the door with trembling hands. Yusra sank onto the couch and grabbed the remote.

Lucien sat in the armchair next to her, staring at her hand holding the remote.

"Are you okay?"

Yusra's eyes stayed glued to the screen, offering a gentle nod in response. Headlines murmured in a continuous, suffocating loop.

"Relocation initiatives expanded on the southern border. Violators will be arrested on the spot."

"Muslims attempt to erase Christianity — Vaughn announces mandatory Christian prayer in public schools."

"New Jersey enacts strict attire requirements. Violations will result in immediate arrest."

Yusra shut the television off. She bowed her head into her palms and breathed soft, shaking sobs into the quiet. Lucien sat beside her, stiff and uncertain. Comfort wasn't something he was good at. After a moment's hesitation, he reached out and gave her covered shoulder a gentle tap, the closest thing to reassurance he could manage, then immediately recoiled, folding into himself.

"I'm so sorry, Yusra," he whispered.

She looked up, cheeks damp, and managed a small, aching smile.

"It's not your fault, Lucien."

Yusra wiped her face with the back of her sleeve, steadying her breath. Only the sound of her shaken inhales could be heard within the silence.. That was when Mercury padded into the room.

The little cat paused in the doorway, tail swaying once. He studied her, really studied her, with those clever amber eyes. Then, he crossed the room, hopped onto the couch, and curled himself against Yusra's hip. She blinked, startled.

"Hi, sweetheart," she whispered.

Mercury headbutted her ribs, then pressed his forehead against her thigh before settling into a loaf. His purr rumbled softly, a grounding vibration. It was the gentlest insistence in the world: You're safe.

Yusra's breath trembled. She placed her hand lightly on his back, stroking from shoulders to tail tip. Mercury leaned into her palm, purring louder. Lucien watched from his armchair, something loosening in his chest. He wasn't good with words, but Mercury always understood. Maybe that was enough. Yusra sniffed and gave a soft laugh through her tears.

"He always knows," she said.

Lucien nodded, gaze lowered.

"He does."

A few beats of silence passed, the kind that felt shared rather than empty. She finally straightened, gathering herself.

"I'm sorry," she murmured. "You just... you didn't need to see all of that."

Lucien shook his head.

"No. That shouldn't have happened to you."

Yusra gave a small, tired smile.

"Welcome to America."

Mercury pressed closer, and she let her fingers drift through his fur again. Slowly, the tear-well slid back behind her composure.

"Thank you," she said softly, not clarifying whether she meant Mercury or Lucien.

Lucien nodded once, quietly.

The weekend passed quickly, swallowing what little comfort Lucien had managed to gather. Monday marked his first day reporting to Section 9.

He arrived troubled. Twice he checked his GPS. Three times he reread the address. He was still staring at a grim, empty alleyway tucked behind an industrial lot, surrounded by forgotten loading bays and cracked asphalt. This couldn't be right.

He shifted the car into park and sat for a long moment, fingers tightening around the steering wheel. Finally, he exhaled, grabbed his scarf, and stepped out. The cold hit him immediately. A harsh, biting wind carved through the narrow alley, turning every metal surface into a low, moaning instrument. Lucien wrapped his scarf over his mouth, breath clouding against the fabric.

He walked toward the only structure with any sign of life, an unmarked brick building with a steel door set into its frame. Two guards flanked it. They were nearly identical to the one who delivered his offer, except dressed entirely in white: white suits, white shoes, white gloves, white rifles, white blank masks. The only color was the dark visor concealing their eyes.

Lucien approached cautiously. His shoes clicked in the cold air. Both guards turned toward him with synchronized precision. One spoke, his voice distorted behind the mask.

"Dr. Tenebris — prompt arrival at 0755 hours."

He handed Lucien a laminated stack: a key card, a crisp white lab coat, a sealed box of latex gloves, then tapped his own badge to a small reader beside the door. The steel door hissed open, releasing a sharp breath of sterilized, recycled air. The guard stepped aside.

"Follow the blue line on the floor. Do not deviate. You will report first to Orientation."

Lucien glanced down. A thin blue stripe, bright against the gray concrete, stretched into a long hallway beyond the door. He swallowed, adjusted his grip on the lab coat, and stepped inside as the door sealed behind him with a hydraulic thud.

The hall was colder than the alley outside. Harsh fluorescent lights cast everything in an anemic wash. The blue line beneath his feet glowed faintly, almost humming, leading him down a row of sealed doors. None had labels. Some had reinforced panels. One had faint scratches across the metal. Every door they passed felt alive with secrecy. Lucien tried not to look too closely, but one door, a tall, reinforced slab, caught his lingering gaze.

A guard immediately barked through his modulator:

"Eyes forward, Dr. Tenebris."

Lucien jerked his attention back to his path.

"Sorry," he murmured.

His escort did not respond. They approached a pair of illuminated sliding doors marked:

ORIENTATION – AUTHORIZED PERSONNEL ONLY

The guard stopped beside him.

"Present your card."

Lucien did. The panel beeped, and the doors parted with a hiss. Inside the Orientation stood a single stainless-steel table, a set of terminals, and a large screen displaying:

WELCOME
SECTION 9 – SUBLEVEL 4
ONBOARDING: DR. LUCIEN TENEBRIS

No greeter.
No supervisor.
No human presence at all.

Lucien exhaled, tension falling from his shoulders. In a strange way, the anonymity felt... safer. He didn't have to perform, or make eye contact, or stumble over introductions. It was clinical. Clear. Predictable. A soft chime sounded. The screen flickered, then shifted to a new prompt:

INSERT KEY CARD TO BEGIN.

Lucien slid his card into the reader. Another chime. Then a synthetic voice, perfectly smooth, genderless, eerily calm, filled the room.

"Welcome, Dr. Tenebris. Orientation will now begin."

A series of bullet points appeared:

• Your access level: B-1
• Your primary assignment: Neural Yield Analysis
• Your workspace: Lab 4B
• Your permissible zones: Blue-lined corridors only
• Do not attempt entry into red or black zones at any time
• Deviations from escort protocol will result in corrective measures

Lucien blinked at the phrasing. "Corrective measures" felt unnecessarily vague. Another screen came up.

"Please review your responsibilities."

A digital document loaded. Pages upon pages of dense, bureaucratic jargon:

• "Trauma compound stabilization"

- "Voluntary neural interface procedure oversight"
- "Contact protocol for B-tier subjects"
- "Emergency contamination response"

Lucien skimmed the terms but didn't fully comprehend them. The terminology felt specialized, and the explanations offered nothing but more jargon. Still, no one walked in. Still, no one spoke except the computer. In some ways, that was preferable. He didn't have to interact. He didn't have to decode subtle cues or facial expressions. The walls didn't stare back at him. No one demanded small talk.

Just data.
Just procedures.
Just clear expectations.

He let himself breathe. Even if part of him wondered why not a single human being was responsible for his orientation. The synthetic voice returned:

"Proceed to Lab 4B. Follow the blue line. Do not deviate."

The doors opened automatically. Lucien stepped into the hallway. The blue line illuminated beneath his feet.

Every corner he turned, white-masked guards stood silent, still as mannequins. None turned to look at him. None addressed him. None acknowledged him beyond the faint mechanical tilt of their heads as he passed.

It was impersonal to the point of being surreal.

Lucien found comfort in it. No eyes on him. No questions. No social pressure. Just quiet corridors and clear instructions.

He tapped his card at the door marked:

LAB 4B — AUTHORIZED ACCESS

The room hissed open. Inside was a pristine, untouched
workspace with metallic counters, sealed containers, gleaming
equipment, and a workstation with his name already printed on
the screen. Everything was orderly. Predictable. Silent.

It was, frankly, ideal.

Lucien hung his lab coat on a hook, pressed gloved fingers to the
cold countertop, and let out a long breath.

This was his domain now. Even if the silence felt too thick. Even if
the air felt too sterilized. Even if the guards outside felt more like
sentries than colleagues. He told himself it was fine. Better than
fine. It was everything he had asked for.

A small panel on the wall flickered with a final message:

BEGINNING WORK CYCLE 001
PLEASE WAIT FOR MATERIAL DELIVERY

Then fell silent. He was alone. Completely alone. Section 9
seemed designed to keep it that way.

Lucien set his box down beside the workstation, the faint hum of
machinery filling the sterile room. Everything was pristine,
untouched. It felt like stepping into a lab preserved in time,
waiting just for him. That was when he noticed the binder. It sat
in the center of the table, slate-gray with a glossy finish, the Section
9 emblem embossed on the cover. A small label on the spine read:

"SUBJECT CATEGORIES — GENERAL OVERVIEW (FOR
RESEARCH STAFF)"

Lucien frowned. He flipped open the cover. A set of laminated graphics greeted him, polished, color-coded diagrams reminiscent of medical school charts mixed with corporate wellness infographics. Clean lines. Smiling silhouettes. Soft blue and green accents meant to soothe. He turned the first page.

An image showed the same white-suited, white-masked guards who guided him through the hallways, though posed like stock-photo models instead of silent sentries.

T-Regime: Trauma Response Security Unit
Designation: Specialist personnel trained in containment, medical escort, and safety compliance.
Role: Ensuring a controlled environment for ongoing research studies.
Additional Responsibilities:
• Recruitment of Bhuvaha volunteers through behavioral identifiers
• Observation of high-yield emotional profiles in public and clinical settings
• Secure transfer of qualifying participants to Section 9 study sites
• De-escalation and transport of distressed or noncompliant subjects
Classification: Tapaha (non-experimental)

Lucien paused. Tapaha?

No one defined the word. The binder didn't either. It simply listed it as a fact, as though he should already know.

He flipped the page.

This page looked... reverent. Golden borders. Posed silhouettes. A tone that felt almost religious.

"Janaha are elite adult participants whose neural profiles exhibit extraordinary memory density and recall capacity. Their contributions provide high-yield samples vital to trauma-compound research. They are compensated generously. Access to Janaha data requires elevated clearance."

Lucien exhaled, impressed.

Extraordinary memory density? That was exactly the kind of profile needed for complex neural chemical mapping. The term donors implied voluntary contribution. He imagined dignified adults signing up to help refine compounds that could one day alleviate trauma responses in millions.

It made sense. It sounded humane.

He flipped the page again.

A single note. No graphics. No smiling silhouettes. Just one sterile sentence:

"Tapaha personnel fulfill specialized internal roles and are not part of the research population."

Lucien blinked, slightly frustrated. What specialized roles? Why so vague? He flipped back to the T-Regime page. Tapaha again. The white-masked guards. Were they a military classification? Medical technicians? Something internal but not part of the study?

He stared at the word, trying to place it, but it had no context, no explanation. The binder assumed he understood these categories already. He didn't.

The binder, however, was professional, scientific, logically organized. He trusted it. He told himself he'd learn more later. Another page listed sample collection procedures for Bhuvaha volunteers and Janaha "donors." He paused. Another new term? Bhuvaha? This page was the only one to make mention of whatever class these people were. Everything read like a medical ethics document. Everything looked legitimate. Everything felt safe.

Lucien closed the binder slowly. The screen hums softly behind him. A gentle chime sounds from the wall panel:

"Material delivery en route."

Lucien adjusts his lab coat, unaware that the label on the incoming tray reads:

C-59 — HIGH-YIELD

He doesn't notice. He's too focused on preparing his instruments. He feels steady, proud, and ready to begin meaningful work.

The fluorescent lights buzz. A faint vibration passes through the floor, metal shifting beneath him. Lucien doesn't register it. He's already reaching for a pipette. The screen behind him flickers. The hum deepens.

VI

Malrick Vaughn entered through a secret passage to the entrance of visitation, a sub-unit of section 9 –- one way glass windows on every wall. He is met by a T-Regime guard, behind him a wide array of animal masks for the taking. A muffled voice meets Vaughn upon arrival from behind the T-Regime mask.

"Good afternoon, Mister President. An honor."

"As it should be."

"What animal would you like to don today, sir?"

Vaughn surveyed the table of animal masks, yet was fixated on one upon his arrival.

"The lion mask. Seems appropriate for the second coming of Christ."

"Of course, sir."

The T-Regime guard gingerly hands Vaughn the lion mask. Vaughn grazes his masked thumb across the artwork, whiskers poking out from the muzzle, a full mane. He slips the mask on and enters visitation.

In visitation, he is met by 4 others – the giraffe with his teenage companion, the elephant, and the zebra. The giraffe's eyes avert away from his captive and onto the president.

"Always an honor when the lion can accompany our ventures."

Vaughn nods, finding his seat in the velvety lined throne at the center of the room. The zebra speaks.

"And who will be the lucky contestant of solitary confinement today?"

Vaughn watches the room. Crane always entered before the victims – a master at crafting torture. Vaughn knew he chose wisely when appointing the Janaha to invoke torture onto the Bhuvaha.

The hiss of hydraulics signaled the start of the next cycle. A red light blinked above the one-way glass wall. The visitation room fell quiet. Behind the glass, the solitary confinement chamber brightened, stark white, surgical, merciless. At its center stood Crane. Even without seeing his face, Vaughn always knew his posture: spine straight, head tilted slightly down, hands folded with ritualistic precision, his sleeked blindingly blonde hair gleaming against the overhead lights.

Black gloves.
Black mask.
Black suit.
The perfect Janaha silhouette.

On the tray beside him lay an arrangement of tools that could've belonged to a sculptor or a surgeon or a butcher. Crane selected them the way musicians selected instruments—intimate, deliberate.

Vaughn shivered. God had truly blessed him with this man.

Two guards dragged the young girl into the chamber.

A tiny gasp rose from her throat as she stumbled forward. The fluorescent lights washed her skin pale, making the dried blood on her cheek appear almost black. She couldn't have been older than fourteen. That trembling, stubborn flicker of defiance in her eyes made Vaughn's pulse quicken. He always liked them with a little bite.

She was a nobody. The uncertainty made it sweeter.

Crane did not look at the girl. He continued arranging his tools, aligning them in a perfect fan, the metal glinting like scripture. The zebra leaned forward. "He's starting." The elephant adjusted his mask, pulling in a breath of anticipation, but the lion — the president — stilled.

Vaughn's gloved fingers tightened around the armrests of his velvet throne. His breath warmed the inside of the lion muzzle. His heartbeat thudded in his ears, echoing like a drumline behind his teeth.

Then the girl lifted her head. Her eyes, wide, wet, utterly terrified, snapped to Vaughn through the glass, as if she sensed him watching. As if she knew him. Her lower lip trembled, reopening the split. Blood welled there, bright and warm. Vaughn inhaled sharply. Heat shot through him. Familiar, addictive, sacred.

"Mm," the giraffe murmured. "Looks like the lion likes this one."

Vaughn didn't answer. He rose from the throne. The room quieted.

Behind the glass, Crane finally turned to face the girl. He touched her cheek with one black-gloved finger, turning her face toward him, examining her split lip with a kind of reverence.

Vaughn swayed.

That tiny smear of blood glinted under the lights. Crane wiped it clean with a pad of gauze, then placed the soiled cloth neatly on the tray. Vaughn's breath fogged the inside of the lion mask. He pressed a palm to the glass.

The giraffe chuckled nervously. "Easy, sir. He hasn't even started yet."

Vaughn felt it. The spiral. The hunger. The scripture written in marrow. His voice trembled through the mask.

"Open the auxiliary door."

The zebra stiffened. "Sir? You've never—"

"I said open it."

A keypad beeped somewhere in the corner of the visitation room. The side access door at the base of the glass wall unlatched with a heavy mechanical clunk. Vaughn stepped toward it slowly, breath ragged.

"Sir, you're entering the confined zone—" the elephant warned.

Vaughn didn't look back.

"I am the lion," he said softly. "I do not watch. I consume."

He slipped through the door. Crane's head snapped up inside the solitary chamber, sensing motion. He didn't expect anyone to enter. No one ever entered. Not during the ritual. A shadow fell across the white floor as Vaughn crossed the threshold. Crane froze mid-gesture, gloved hand suspended above his tray of tools.

The girl whimpered.

Vaughn approached her slowly, reverently, like she was an altar.

Vaughn stared at the girl, the lion mask inches from her trembling face. Through the one-way glass behind him, the spectators watched in reverent silence. Crane stood inside the solitary chamber, perfectly still, black gloves suspended above his tray of instruments like a paused executioner.

The girl whimpered as Vaughn unclasped his gloves. No one spoke. No president had ever bared their skin in the confinement chamber. The gloves slid off with a whisper, revealing pale, shaking hands. Nothing about what he was about to do was fragile. Vaughn cradled the girl's cheeks in both palms.

She cried out, and it hit him: A Janaha memory invasion.

Not immersion.
Not empathy.
Not travel.

Violation.
Penetration.
Consumption.

Her memories ripped open like raw wounds, spilling into him with violent clarity.

The white walls blurred.
The chamber spun.
Her fear swallowed his senses whole.

Running down an alley.
A hand covering her mouth.
A van door slamming shut.
A needle.
The sound of children crying through vents.
Bright lights.
Her first extraction,
burning, tearing, unbearable—

Vaughn gasped, knees locking as the trauma surged through him in a crashing wave. He leaned in, trembling, and dragged his tongue across her jaw. Her blood, warm, metallic, still rich with unprocessed Redline, hit him like a divine narcotic. The memories detonated harder.

A boot against her ribs.
A guard laughing.
Metal restraints.
A scream that lasted far too long.

Vaughn moaned. It sounded almost holy. Someone behind the glass whispered, afraid, "He's taking on too much—"

Crane watched in horror, his voice struggling to leave his lips, controlled but edged with warning.

"President Vaughn. Janaha memory absorption is not meant to be taken at full trauma potency."

Vaughn ignored him. His fingers dug deeper into the girl's cheeks, forcing the connection open wider. Her sobbing vibrated against his palms. The trauma, fresh, unfiltered, electric, lashed him again and again. He laughed. Soft. Breathless. A terrible, ecstatic sound. Crane stepped forward, rigid.

"Sir. Release her. Now."

Vaughn lifted his head. His pupils were blown wide, nearly black. Blood smeared his mouth. He looked euphoric. Anointed. Unhinged.

"Do you feel it?" he whispered. "Her agony... it's a revelation."

The girl sagged in his grip, barely conscious. Vaughn stroked her lip again, gathering more blood, tasting it with a shaking exhale as another violent burst of memory slammed into his mind. He shuddered.

"I need more," he whispered.

Crane's posture sharpened. The spectators behind the glass went utterly still. Vaughn's fingers trembled against the girl's cheeks. Her breath was ragged, shallow, her eyes rolling back as he held her in that Janaha mind-lock.

"President Vaughn," Crane warned, voice dropping into something sharp. "You are exceeding threshold. Release her."

Vaughn wasn't listening. He tightened his grip.

The connection tore fully open, a violent conduit, memories ripping through both of them at once. The girl screamed. Her body arched, spine bowing, limbs shaking in involuntary spasms. Vaughn inhaled, shuddering, as fresh trauma spilled into him like molten glass: panic, abandonment, terror, physical pain, spiritual exhaustion, all slamming into him without filter. He felt her dying terror and called it euphoria.

Crane lunged forward, grabbing Vaughn's wrist, but the shock of Vaughn's bare skin sent Crane staggering back as if burned. Vaughn's consciousness was a storm, chaotic and ravenous, and even Crane couldn't touch him without recoil.

"Sir, let go of her!" Crane barked.

Vaughn moaned instead, low and guttural, as the girl's last reservoirs of trauma unlocked. Her memories shredded like paper in a hurricane. Her breath hitched. Once. Twice. Vaughn pulled her face closer, pressing his forehead to hers.

He whispered, trembling,
"Speak to me. One last prophecy."

There was nothing left to give. No fear. No resistance. A collapsing consciousness flailing in darkness. Her body convulsed violently, and then dropped limp, dead weight in Vaughn's hands. The chamber went silent.

Behind the glass, someone gasped. Another masked spectator vomited quietly into a velvet-lined receptacle. Crane moved fast now, grabbing Vaughn's shoulder and wrenching him backward. Vaughn staggered, still half inside her mind, still shaking as the last flickers of her dying trauma evaporated from his bloodstream.

He stared at her body. Not with horror. Not even with regret. Only hunger. He raised his blood-smeared hand to his mouth and licked the last trace of her memory from his thumb. A single whisper escaped him, a believer tasting divinity.

"...more..."

Crane's mask tilted sharply.

"Sir, she's gone. You've drained her."

Vaughn did not look away from the girl's corpse.

"She was weak," he murmured. "God will send me another."

The spectators stepped back, instinctively recoiling. Something had changed. Not in the chamber. In the president. For the first time, his appetite had surpassed the system designed to contain it. Crane swallowed hard.

"We'll need to dispose of the body immediately."

One of the spectators, voice quivering under a zebra mask, whispered.

"This rate of... depletion... is unsustainable. We'll run out of subjects."

Vaughn turned, slow and eerie, toward the glass.

"No," he said calmly from behind the lion mask. "You'll simply acquire more."

He stepped toward Crane, breath still ragged, eyes blown wide with the aftershock of Janaha overdose.

"Build the proper facilities to manage... casualties."

Crane froze. The spectators understood. This was the night the Incineration Room was conceived from hunger. After this moment, the casualty rate in Section 9 would triple. Victims would "expire" more often under interrogation. Janaha consumption would escalate into frenzy. Bodies would pile faster than they could be buried.

And Vaughn—

Vaughn would never again settle for distilled Redline. He wanted it raw. Living. Screaming. He looked down at the corpse one last time. A quiet, chilling smile formed behind the lion mask.

"We'll call it purification," he said softly. "A righteous cleansing of the unworthy."

Crane said nothing. He knew: This was not an isolated incident. This was the new order.

VII

Yusra spent many evenings preparing dinner for her and Lucien, an addition to life that Lucien quite enjoyed. Rather than meeting the scent of burnt popcorn he'd snack on, he came home to scents that filled him with warmth all the way deep into his chest. This night brought a welcome addition to Yusra's cooking. She began humming.

Lucien pretended to focus on formulae in his assignment with Section 9, but he found his ears perking, searching the melody, how it flowed, its intervals. His fingers twitched slightly against the table, playing on an invisible keyboard beneath them. He didn't recognize the tune, not entirely, but something about the descending line in the middle felt familiar enough to make his attention snag.

Yusra glanced over her shoulder, caught him listening, and her smile tugged crooked and knowing.

"You've got that look," she teased gently.

He blinked. "What look?"

"The one where you pretend you don't hear anything, but you're analyzing every note." She swirled the wooden spoon in the pot and hummed a bar more clearly, lilting, effortless. ""It's Fairuz," she says. "Nassam Alayna. My mother used to hum it."

Lucien's eyes lowered back to his paperwork. "Ah."

The response was too quick, the type that revealed how intently he'd been listening. She chuckled softly and turned back to the stove. He tried to resume reading. He really did, but the melody filtered through the apartment, warm, soft, impossibly human, and something in his chest tightened around it, filing each interval away with the precision of someone who didn't know how to ignore the things he cared about.

A few minutes later, she called from the kitchen.

"Dinner's ready."

Lucien rose almost too quickly, not only eager for a delicious meal his dearest friend prepared for them, but also searching for grounding in the midst of his wandering thoughts. They sat at the small wooden table they'd claimed as theirs, Mercury weaving between their ankles, hopeful for scraps. Yusra served the stew, humming the tail end of the Fairuz melody without realizing she'd slipped back into it.

Lucien noticed every recurrence.

They ate in that easy quiet they'd grown accustomed to, punctuated by Yusra's soft commentary about the recipe and Lucien's unexpectedly earnest questions about the spices she used.

Mercury eventually hopped into Lucien's lap, curling against his stomach as if the purr might soothe whatever he was trying to bury beneath his analytical focus.

When they finished, Yusra washed while Lucien dried the dishes. It was a ritual neither of them had established on purpose, but one they followed naturally, both moving around the kitchen with the kind of unspoken coordination that only forms when two people have settled into each other's rhythms.

Only after she disappeared down the hallway with a stack of papers to grade did Lucien drift toward the piano, as if pulled by the thread of a melody that had been woven through his entire evening.

Hours later, when she's grading papers in the bedroom, a thin thread of music drifts down the hallway. A hesitant left hand. An uncertain melodic line. The tune he claimed not to hear. A single melodic line. Searching. Repeating. Lucien at the piano playing her mother's song as if uncovering it slowly, like pieces of a puzzle he wasn't sure he had permission to solve.

Yusra paused in the doorway, listening with a tender, almost disbelieving smile. He didn't look up. He didn't need to. He was learning her in the only language he trusted. She stayed in the doorway a moment longer before speaking. The upright piano in the corner had always struck Yusra as one of those inherited house relics, something Lucien had never mentioned and never touched. She'd nearly convinced herself it was decorative.

"I knew you understood music," she said softly, "but... I didn't know you *played*."

Lucien froze for a fraction of a second, fingers suspended just above the next chord.

"I don't," he said quickly. "Not really."

"That isn't 'not really.'" Her smile deepened, warm and gentle. "That's someone who's studied something. Perhaps even loved it."

His ears flushed a quiet red, the kind that showed just at the tips.

"I'm... only mapping what I heard."

Mercury hopped onto the bench then, curling himself unapologetically into Lucien's lap. Lucien stiffened, then softened, one hand drifting to the cat's back like an instinct he couldn't fight.

"He approves," Yusra said.

"Of the intrusion?" Lucien muttered.

"Of you playing."

She stepped fully into the room now, not crowding him, just present.

"Why didn't you ever tell me you knew piano?"

He hesitated, searching, an analytical pause of his.

"It didn't seem relevant."

"Lucien," she said, sitting lightly on the arm of the sofa, "you're playing one of my mother's songs."

That silenced him. Not out of guilt. Out of something more like... overwhelmed honesty.

"I was only... curious about the intervals," he murmured.

Then, as if hearing himself aloud triggered a recoil, Lucien's hands stilled. Completely. They hovered over the keys for a heartbeat, then withdrew into his lap with abrupt precision, the way someone might hide a wound or a secret.

Mercury let out a faint chirp of protest at the sudden stillness. Lucien kept his eyes fixed on the piano lid, jaw rigid, the faint flush at his ears darkening.

"I shouldn't have—" he started, but the sentence collapsed under its own weight. "It wasn't meant to be..."

He exhaled sharply. "Heard."

Yusra softened, her expression shifting instantly to reassurance.

"Lucien," she said quietly, "you didn't do anything wrong."

He shook his head once, a tiny movement, almost imperceptible. "I wasn't trying to... intrude on something personal."

"You weren't."

Her voice held no pressure, only warmth. "You were being yourself. That isn't an intrusion."

His fingers curled tightly against his palms, knuckles paling. "I shouldn't have touched the piano," he said softly, embarrassed in a way that went bone-deep, not because he lacked skill, but because what he'd revealed wasn't meant to be seen.

Yusra placed a gentle hand on his covered shoulder, offering a small, steady grin before sitting in a chair near the piano.

"There was a time when things weren't so difficult," she began, voice soft but sure. "Life was a little less traumatic. I knew far less than what I know now. That's honestly the only way the story of Adam and Eve has ever made sense to me, not because God was punishing them for disobeying, but because He was protecting them from what knowledge costs. The more we learn, the more we experience... the greater the toll it can take on us. Sometimes it can harm us."

Lucien turned slightly, lifting an eyebrow, reserving judgment but listening. Yusra continued.

"I don't know that you realize the gift you've given me by taking the time to recreate something from my mother's daily routines. That song... it takes me back to Eden. Back to innocence, to childhood, before I had any grasp of war or hatred." Her voice thinned with emotion, but did not tremble. "You brought me back to Eden."

Lucien slumped forward, forehead nearly brushing the fallboard.

"I don't play very well with people watching."

Her smile softened. "Would you prefer I turn around? Or even leave the room, if that would help you feel at ease?"

He hesitated.

"I don't want you to leave. Just... turn around."

Yusra nodded and swiveled her chair without another word. The trust in that small gesture settled the air between them. Lucien closed his eyes, his fingers returning to the keys with slow, deliberate intention. The melody emerged again, gentler this time, shaped with care, almost reverence, his hands painting the Arabic text so beloved to Yusra.

She smiled, unseen, with a warmth no one in his life had probably ever offered him. Not for this. Not for something so human.

VIII

The tunnels beneath the facility hummed faintly, a low mechanical drone that rattled through Lucien's ribcage. He kept his gaze low, fingers brushing the fabric at the hem of his sleeve in a soft, rhythmic stim as he approached the main junction. The familiar route to his lab was blocked.

A T-Regime guard stood before the sealed passage, rifle angled across his chest. His entire uniform was white, mask, armor, gloves, an absence of color that made him feel less like a man and more like a surgical instrument.

"Tenebris," the guard said flatly. "Detour. Your sector is not authorized today."

Lucien swallowed the rise of unease, nodded once, and turned down the indicated corridor. This hallway was different, narrower, the air sharper. Doors lined each side in a neat, clinical row. Most were shut. One wasn't. The slightest crack, enough for light to slip through. Lucien's steps hesitated, unwilling curiosity tugging against his better instincts. He glanced inside.

A line of children, maybe eight to thirteen, stood in perfect formation. Uniforms pressed to rigidity. Hands clasped behind small backs. Eyes forward, unblinking. Their stillness felt wrong, like mannequins posed with too much precision. His breath shuddered.

Then one of them moved.

A girl, dark hair falling to the middle of her back, turned her head just enough for her eyes to find his. Black eyes. Silent, watchful, impossibly alert. A jolt shot through him, too sudden, too intimate. Lucien's gaze dropped immediately. His heart thrashed in his throat in that odd way it sometimes did when emotion hit too quickly. He pressed his thumb to the ridge of his index finger, one, two, three—to steady himself.

He walked on. Let the government guard its secrets. His job required him not to see.

He had long stopped trying to understand Section 9. The facility functioned like a living organism that was sterile, rhythmic, unnervingly precise. After the first several weeks, Lucien had adapted the way anyone did: quietly, efficiently, without unnecessary thought.

People didn't last here if they asked questions. People lasted if they focused.

He focused.

He followed the blue line to Lab 4B, the familiar hum of the building pulsing gently beneath his feet. The air always smelled the same, chemical, cold, vaguely metallic, but after enough time, even the wrongness had its own predictability. Lucien took comfort in that. Predictability worked on him the way music theory did. It stilled the static.

Today, though, something tugged at him. The sight of the children lingered in the back of his mind, distorting the edges of the routine he'd finally mastered. ROTC kids, he told himself. Junior recruits. Something benign. Something structured. There had to be an explanation.

He set his things down in the lab. The lights above him buzzed once. Just once. A flicker he'd seen before, a flicker he ignored before, but today it caught on him like a snagged thread. The intercom chimed instantly:

"Power recalibration complete."

Lucien exhaled, steadying his hands against the counter. He'd heard that line countless times. The exact same cadence. The exact same artificial warmth. Enough repetition would make anything feel normal.

He worked.

Pipettes. Vials. Temperature adjustments. The familiar routine smoothed his nerves until the world narrowed into solvable equations.

At 1300, a pair of T-Regime guards escorted a stretcher past the lab window. Not unusual. He'd seen it a dozen times before. A white sheet. No voice beneath it. No reason offered.

The same announcement followed:

"Subject transfer in progress."

Normally, that phrase rolled right off him. Today, it stuck.

He adjusted his equipment too forcefully and had to steady the rack with both hands. He told himself it didn't matter. That the children had simply unsettled him in a way he didn't expect. That he was overanalyzing.

Routine. Focus. Breathe.

At 1500, the monthly sterilization cycle kicked in. The vents exhaled a cloud of antiseptic air so sharp it carved through his sinuses. Beneath the sting of bleach was something sweeter. Warmer. Something like copper and flowers, impossible and out of place. That smell had hit him before, faint as a ghost. He dismissed it like always. He had never once found the courage to ask about it.

As always, the intercom chimed:

"Please remain at your workstation during decontamination."

He did. He always did.

By late evening, most personnel had cleared the sublevel. The hall outside his lab was still. Almost peaceful. Lucien preferred this hour. The hum softened, the fluorescent harshness dimmed just slightly, and the world around him felt manageable, contained. He leaned into his work, falling into the rhythm that numbed the unease, the quiet that let him forget the eyes of the girl in the hallway, too old for her small face.

For a moment, it felt like the day might settle back into predictability after all.

Then, softly, almost politely, the door to Lab 4B creaked open. Lucien froze.

The girl from the hallway stood framed in the doorway. Not in her starched uniform now, but in fleece pajamas patterned with plaid. The incongruity jolted him more than her presence. She shouldn't be here. She shouldn't be unguarded. She shouldn't look this... childlike. Her voice was small but steady.

"Who are you?"

Lucien blinked at her. Speech took a moment to arrive; it always did when emotions came first.

"I... could ask you the same," he managed.

She lowered her gaze to the floor.

"T-853."

The number tugged at him. Familiar in shape, not in meaning. He'd glimpsed strings like it stamped onto equipment crates or embedded in guard ID tags, but never spoken aloud by a child. Something about it didn't add up, a faint wrongness settling in his stomach. He forced himself to rationalize it.

Section 9 labeled everything, even training groups, probably. It couldn't mean anything else.

He glanced at her hair, black, soft, almost luminous in the sterile lab light.

"That won't do," he said quietly.

She looked up, confused.

"If you'll allow it," Lucien continued, "I'd rather call you..."
He hesitated, searching for something gentle, something human.
"...Raven."

The girl blinked. A small, uncertain breath escaped her, something between surprise and relief. No smile. Not yet, but something softened. Something that might one day become her name. Or be replaced by another. Something Section 9 might take from her. Something she might reclaim.

For now, though, she was Raven. Neither of them would understand it yet, but this was the first moment they became tethered.

For a long moment, neither of them moved. Lucien stood by his workstation, shoulders stiff, one gloved hand hovering awkwardly over a beaker. The girl lingered in the doorway, small feet planted on the sterile tile, her plaid pajamas glaringly soft against the cold blue light.

Children weren't supposed to wander into restricted sections. Children weren't supposed to wander *anywhere* without permission.

She didn't look afraid. She simply looked... curious.

Lucien cleared his throat, the sound too loud in the quiet lab.

"You shouldn't be here," he said gently.

She stepped inside anyway. Her eyes drifted over the glass instruments, the glowing vials, the metallic tubing. It reminded Lucien briefly of a bird stepping into a foreign landscape, cautious steps, head tilting in quick, precise movements.

"What is this place?" she asked.

"A laboratory," he murmured.

She frowned.

"What does that mean?"

Lucien blinked. He wasn't used to being asked questions. At least, not by people who actually wanted answers.

"It means I study things," he said slowly. "Reactions. Functions. How one thing becomes another."

She approached one of the counters, her gaze softening at the sight of a cooling coil's gentle vapor cloud.

"Do you make weapons?" she asked.

"No." Then, after a beat: "At least, not to my knowledge."

The child held his words in her small hands, weighing them in a way most adults didn't bother to. Lucien found himself watching her, strangely unable to look away. Something about her presence didn't overwhelm him the way people usually did. She was quiet in the right ways. Observant in the right ways. Her gaze didn't press against him, didn't demand anything he didn't know how to give. It felt... tolerable. Almost grounding.

She circled toward his central table. Lucien instinctively shifted a beaker out of her reach as a reflex.

"You're not frightened," he said. "Most children are."

"I'm not like most children."

Lucien almost smiled. Almost. Before he could find a response, the overhead speakers crackled faintly, a burst of static, followed by distant, clipped footsteps echoing through the corridor. The girl stiffened. Lucien recognized the shift — shoulders tensed, spine straightening just enough to hide the fear behind discipline. He had seen soldiers do it endlessly. He hated seeing it on her.

Another voice drifted down the hall:

"—T-853? Where did she go?"

Lucien's pulse kicked. He wasn't a rebellious man by nature. His instincts bent toward survival, routine, anonymity. Something sharpened inside him then, a thin, bright line of protectiveness he didn't fully understand. He lowered his voice.

"You weren't supposed to wander, were you?"

She shook her head.

"Did you run?"

"...I didn't want to sleep," she whispered.

Lucien exhaled slowly. Footsteps grew louder. He made a decision before he had time to question it.

"This way," he murmured, motioning her toward the side door used for supply deliveries. He keyed in a manual override, and the panel slid open just enough for a small body to slip through. Dim emergency light spilled into a narrow service corridor.

"Follow this passage," he instructed, kneeling to her level without quite realizing he had done so. "It loops behind the barracks wall."

She hesitated. Her dark eyes held his again, steady, searching, almost unnervingly perceptive for someone so young. He had the uncanny feeling she was memorizing him, filing away the shape of him in a place she did not yet understand.

"Thank you," she whispered.

Lucien swallowed.

"Go. Quietly."

She slipped into the corridor. The door eased shut behind her with a soft hydraulic sigh just as a pair of guards passed the intersection outside his lab. Lucien turned back to his workstation, trying to look as though he had never been interrupted, as though his heart wasn't thundering.

The guards' voices echoed just beyond the glass:

"She couldn't have gone far."

"Search every unauthorized wing."

Lucien stared at his beaker, hands trembling faintly. For reasons he couldn't name, couldn't articulate even to himself, he knew he would do it again. Help her. Protect her. Choose her. Even before he knew who she would become. Even before she had a name.

Lucien returned home to find Yusra waiting with a plate of warm ka'ek on the small wooden table, Mercury curled loyally at her feet. The second he stepped inside, she saw it. His exhaustion had stripped away every layer of masking he normally kept in place. Fear flickered plain across his face.

Her smile faltered. "Lucien... what's wrong?"

He blinked at her, almost startled, as if he hadn't expected another person to exist in the room at all. His thoughts buzzed so fiercely she could almost feel them in the air.

"T-853…" he whispered.

"What?"

"That was her name."

"Whose name?"

What came out of him next wasn't language so much as a tangle of broken syllables, panicked and aimless. Yusra rose immediately, placing both hands firmly on his shoulders. Her touch was steady, warm, grounding. She breathed in deeply and let it out.

"Hey," she murmured, gently shushing him. "Match me."

He followed, hesitant at first, then syncing with her rhythm. Inhale. Exhale. His shoulders eased by a fraction.

She offered him a small, reassuring smile. "Let's get some food in you."

Lucien barely looked at the ka'ek before tearing into it, shoveling pieces into his mouth with frantic efficiency. Yusra bit back a soft laugh.

"Remember to chew," she said lightly.

He obeyed, chewing mechanically, swallowing hard. The plate was empty within minutes.

Yusra touched her chest again, a quiet gesture between them.

"One more breath for me."

Lucien inhaled, deeper this time, then let it go. When she finally met his eyes, hers were threaded with worry and patience in equal measure.

"Good," she whispered. "Now... you mentioned T-853?"

Lucien nodded, rubbing at his wrist in a small, anxious circle. "She called herself that. T-853. I gave her a different name, Raven. It just felt way too... inhumane to refer to her by a series of letters and numbers."

Yusra leaned forward. "Have you seen codes like that before?"

"Yes." He exhaled shakily. "They use that format for the T-Regime. All numbers starting with T. The guards who walk me through the hallways. The ones in white." He swallowed. "In my onboarding, their binder had an entire page labeled T-Regime. Next to it... the word Tapaha."

Yusra repeated it quietly. "Tapaha."

Lucien nodded. "It's their classification, but they didn't define it." His voice pinched with frustration. "The page acted like I should already know. Just a line that said 'Classification: Tapaha (non-experimental).' Like that meant something."

"And it didn't?" she asked gently.

"It meant nothing," he admitted. "Nothing I could make sense of. No explanation. No context. The next page only said, 'Tapaha personnel fulfill specialized internal roles and are not part of the research population.'" He shook his head. "That's all. No definitions. No descriptions. Just a word."

"Now a child has the same kind of designation," Yusra said.

Lucien's eyes flickered. "Exactly. I've only ever seen adults with T-numbers. Full-grown guards in white masks. Never a child." His voice tightened. "She shouldn't have that label. Not at that age."

Yusra's face softened with a slow, careful concern. "Do you think she's part of the T-Regime?"

"I don't know," Lucien whispered. "But if 'Tapaha' is tied to those guards, then why would a child use the same prefix?"

Yusra let the silence sit, heavy and thoughtful. "Lucien… what was she like?"

He breathed out, eyes unfocused as the memory tightened behind them. "She stood like them. Not exactly, but close. Controlled. Waiting. Listening for commands I couldn't hear." He rubbed his palms on his pants. "When she looked at me, it felt like she recognized something. I don't know what. It was only a second." He glanced up at Yusra, vulnerable. "I'm probably imagining it."

"Or you noticed something true without having language for it yet," Yusra said softly.

Lucien swallowed. "I don't want to think she's part of something harmful."

Yusra nodded, gentle but firm. "The harm wouldn't come from her."

He exhaled shakily, relief flickering across his features.

She leaned in slightly. "Lucien… why did this disturb you enough to come home shaking?"

He hesitated, then admitted quietly, "Because she didn't look like a guard. She looked like a child someone forgot to protect. She called herself a number like it was the only thing she'd ever been taught."

Yusra leaned forward slightly, elbows braced on her knees, closing the space between them in a way that felt present but not intrusive. She never reached for his hands; she knew he startled at contact, even if neither of them could name the deeper reason why.

"Lucien…"

He stared at the table, breath tight, fingers curled lightly around the fabric of his sleeve. Touch had always been a landmine, overwhelming, unpredictable, sometimes filled with sudden flashes or impressions he could never explain. He didn't know it was memory. He only knew it felt wrong, too loud, too much. He avoided it.

"I can't stop hearing her say it," he said softly.

Yusra's voice gentled. "Then we pay attention. Together."

The line of his shoulders eased just a little. "Okay."

"And Lucien?" she murmured.

He lifted his gaze, guarded but hopeful.

"That word… Tapaha. I want you to tell me everything you remember from onboarding. Even the parts that felt useless."

He nodded, relief and confusion twisting together. "Tomorrow," he whispered.

"Tomorrow," she echoed.

At their feet, Mercury rose from his spot and padded forward, resting his chin on Lucien's ankle, solid, warm, and safe.
Lucien didn't recoil; he never did with Mercury. Animals didn't overwhelm him the way people did. They didn't press or push or flood him with sensations he couldn't categorize.

He exhaled, the smallest bit steadier.

IX

Yusra sat quietly at her desk, waiting for the remaining students to finish their midterms. She had already offered them a small mercy—once they were finished, they were allowed to leave.

Students often spoke fondly of Yusra as their professor. She approached learning objectives with kindness and patience. After all, it isn't a simple task to teach a fish to fly. She wanted her students to crave theology and religious studies, but more importantly, she hoped to guide them toward whatever it was they were destined to pursue.

It was unfortunate, then, how outsiders treated her with such malice. Yusra confidently wore her hijab each day, beginning with a quiet prayer at her desk. Vaughn's administration had already banned attire that was not resonant with Americanized Christianity, but she refused to oblige. Her peers at the university stood alongside her... most of them, at least. Those who didn't made themselves known in the crowds around campus, screaming profanities and slurs at her and anyone else labeled "other."

Yusra refused to let her teachings be white-washed or heavily mistranslated. She treated the Bible as literature, stories meant to guide, not laws meant to bind. She reminded her students that

Jesus spoke in parables. She framed her interpretations as just that: interpretations. She emphasized how often scripture had been distorted or stripped of context to justify harm including slavery and homophobia while conveniently leaving untouched the sins of abuse or exploitation.

Those brave enough to take her courses understood her heart. Those who protested made their presence loud.

The final student handed in their exam. Yusra was alone in her classroom. She shuffled the papers and placed them in her satchel. She missed Lucien's presence at the university; it was difficult not to feel lonely. This was her first year teaching, and though she had survived the semester, she often felt her coworkers regarded her with either disdain or obligation. Lucien was the only one who spoke to her without pretense.

She turned out the lights and stepped into the hall. It was vacant, but the shouts outside bled through the walls.

When she exited the building, she saw a flood of student protesters. Some opposed her teaching, yes, but across the wave of bodies, signs lifted high, each catching her eye in turn:

"NO JUSTICE, NO PEACE!"
"LOVE IS LOVE"
"TRANS RIGHTS ARE HUMAN RIGHTS"
"NO GENOCIDE IN OUR NAME"

The sight filled her with pride.

That pride shifted abruptly into dread.

Prison buses and vans barreled into the crowd, slamming into students. There was no time to even discern if anyone had been injured, or even killed. Cries rose. Tear gas burst in white plumes.

Those caught in the chaos were swept up, dragged, beaten. Rubber bullets gave way to live rounds.

The gas hit her full in the face. She collapsed, curling inward, covering her eyes. Tears streamed uncontrollably. Each inhale tasted of metal and pepper.

Then, as swiftly as they had arrived, the vehicles fled.

The massive crowd dissolved, leaving only counter-protesters chanting Vaughn-approved slogans and a few dazed students stumbling through the haze. A single protest sign lay trampled near her feet: LOVE IS LOVE, smeared with mud and blood.

Yusra forced herself upright, lungs burning, vision blurred. The sudden quiet was worse than the chaos. An instinct rose sharp in her chest: go home.

She clutched her satchel to her body and staggered forward, heart pounding with one desperate thought:

I need to get home. I need to see Lucien.

Yusra swung the door hard upon arrival, looking desperately for Lucien. He was nowhere in sight. She was on the brink of panic when it dawned on her. It was Wednesday. He had to work late at the lab.

She had to wait.

Her patience was thin, if existent at all. Mercury brushed his body against her leg, her hands trembling as she grabbed the remote.

Television. Television should quiet this panic.

She turned it on.

Vaughn's face.

She flinched. "I can't look at him right now!"

She switched the channel.
Vaughn's face.
Switched again.
Vaughn's face.
Again.
Still Vaughn's face.

She was trapped. A rising, helpless fury gripped her chest as she screamed at the TV.

Then Vaughn spoke.

"My fellow co-patriots," he began, his voice warm, rehearsed, poisonous. "Children of this great renewed nation. The time is upon us. We face an enemy not across oceans... but within our very gates."

Yusra froze.

"We will no longer tolerate subversion disguised as compassion. We will no longer allow the liberal disease to infect our families, our churches, our God-ordained order. Anyone breaking protocol will be arrested on the spot. Anyone spreading misinformation will be detained."

His eyes sharpened, an eerie glint behind the smile.

"There are those among you harboring hostages of the state. Traitors hiding in plain sight. They will be found. They will be corrected. They will witness the full measure of my mercy."

He leaned closer to the camera, almost intimate.

"Obedience is mercy. Obedience is salvation. Obey, and you are free. Disobey..." He let the silence hang. "Gather 'em up, boys."

The feed cut abruptly. Static hissed from the speakers.

Yusra's breath caught. The room felt smaller.

Then, without warning, the screen flickered to a new image. A pink cartoon rabbit in a meadow. Round cheeks. Big eyes. A smile too wide. Music chirped as it bounced in place, then began to sing in a high, sugary voice:

"Who's the greatest of them all?
It's Vaughn, our Vaughn! Standing straight and tall!
Our savior has come in our strong and abled man—
If he can't do it, we know no one can!"

Yusra stared, disbelief turning into revulsion.

She grabbed the remote, flipping through channels.

Pink rabbit.
Pink rabbit.
Pink rabbit.
The same fucking pink rabbit.

Another jagged scream tore out of her as she shut the TV off. The remote hit the floor, batteries skittering across the tile. She sank onto the couch, clutching the nearest pillow as her body shook, the tears spilling faster than she could wipe them away.

Her sobbing thinned into quiet shivers, exhaustion settling heavy over her until sleep claimed her.

The house was quiet when Lucien stepped inside. Too quiet.

He shook the cold from his jacket, closing the door with care. The lights in the living room were still on. A pillow lay discarded on the rug, a remote without batteries beside it. The television screen reflected static, the faint hum the only sign it had been shut off in haste.

Then he saw her.

Yusra was curled on the couch, still in her coat, tear tracks dried along her cheeks. Mercury lay at her feet, chin resting protectively on her ankle. She had cried herself into sleep, her breath shallow and uneven.

Lucien's chest tightened.

He approached slowly, lowering himself to the rug beside her. He didn't touch her. He never initiated touch, but he rested a folded blanket over her shoulders, careful not to wake her.

She stirred anyway.

She pushed herself upright, blinking hard. "Lucien?"

The moment she woke, he saw it. Her red, swollen eyes, the tremble in her hands... his expression softened into something pained.

"You've been crying," he whispered.

She almost laughed. It was obvious. "The broadcast... it was on every channel. Vaughn. Then that—rabbit." Her breath hitched. "I couldn't shut it off fast enough."

Lucien approached slowly, as if crossing a fragile landscape. "I'm sorry I wasn't here."

"You couldn't have known."

He lowered himself onto the rug near her, shoulders sagging beneath a heaviness that wasn't just physical. His thumb moved along the seam of his sleeve, his anchor when the world overwhelmed him.

"I had a long day," he murmured. "Everything felt too loud. Too bright. Too... wrong. I didn't want to understand any more of it."

Yusra nodded. She didn't press for more. She could feel in him the same fraying she felt in herself. She reached for the tin of ka'ek she'd set aside before crying herself to sleep and pushed it toward him. "Eat something."

He obeyed out of the same instinct that guided both of them tonight: survival through small rituals.

After a while, she said softly, "You spaced out again."

Lucien rubbed harder at his sleeve. "I'm just tired, and scared, maybe. Everything at the lab feels like a secret I'm getting too close to without meaning to."

Yusra's expression warmed with sympathy. "You're trying to stay human in a place that doesn't allow it," she murmured. "That matters."

He blinked at the compliment, unsure how to receive warmth without flinching from it.

She offered a weak, teasing smile. "Also... your tea still tastes like dirt."

A tiny breath of laughter escaped him. "You make it better."

"I make *everything* better," she said lightly, nudging his foot, and immediately drawing back when she saw him jolt at the unexpected touch. She respected the boundary without a word.

Silence pooled between them, thick but gentle. Yusra leaned her head back against the couch cushion. Her eyes softened in a way that stripped her down to truth.

"Lucien?" she whispered.

He looked down at her.

She was close, not in distance, but in vulnerability. The kind of closeness that asks something without speaking.

"I care about you," she said, voice trembling. "So much."

She leaned in, slowly... carefully... giving him all the space in the world to meet her and lean in.

He didn't. Lucien froze.

His breath snapped short. His chest locked. His entire body recoiled before he could stop it, the couch creaking under the sudden movement.

Yusra's eyes widened, hurt flickering for half a second before compassion quickly smothered it.

"Oh—Lucien—"

He was already breaking.

"I'm sorry—I'm sorry—I can't—"

His hands rubbed together in frantic circles, stimming so hard his shoulders shook.

"I didn't mean to— I just— I can't—"

He curled inward, bracing instinctively for anger, for rejection. Yusra did neither. She lowered herself onto the rug beside him, palms open, gentle, grounded.

"Lucien," she whispered. "Look at me."

He couldn't.

"It's okay," she said. "You didn't do anything wrong."

His breathing faltered.

"I scared you," she murmured. "I'm sorry. I misread the moment."

He swallowed hard. "I didn't want to hurt you."

"You didn't."

"You're not... angry?"

"No," she said immediately. "Not at all."

His voice cracked. "You're not going to leave?"

Her expression softened, warm and steady like a lamp in a power outage.

"Lucien," she murmured, "you're my best friend. Who else is going to eat ka'ek with me at midnight and listen to me complain about my students?"

A fragile, trembling breath escaped him, something like relief wearing the shape of a laugh. She brushed a sesame seed from her knee, voice gentle.

"You don't owe me romance. Or touch. Or anything. That's not how you love. I have never, not once, felt unwanted by you."

He looked at her then, really looked, his eyes bright with emotion he couldn't name. Her voice softened further.

"Can I ask something?"

He nodded weakly.

"Would a hug help? Only if it feels okay. If not, that's truly fine."

Lucien's breath stalled. No one had ever offered him touch like a choice.

"I..." His hands trembled. "Yes. But slow."

"Slow," she promised.

She approached him at half-speed, visible and cautious. He didn't pull away. When her arms wrapped lightly around him, barely there, he stiffened...

Then melted.

His fists unclenched. His breath shuddered. His forehead hovered near her shoulder, just close enough to feel warmth. She held him as long as he needed. When he pulled back, his eyes were wet but steady.

"Thank you," he whispered.

"Always," she said.

She stood, wiping her face. "Let's make better tea," she murmured. "Yours still tastes like you boiled it in a lab."

A faint smile ghosted his lips. For one fragile moment, they both felt safe.

X

The late shift had drained the world of color. The hum of the
ventilation system vibrated the lab counters, steady as a pulse.
Lucien measured the final compounds into their vials, sealed
them, and slid them into the metal transfer window. As always,
there were no hands waiting on the other side to collect them, only
the mechanical hiss as the window shut.

Predictable. Comforting, in its own sterile way.

He shrugged out of his lab coat, shoulders slumping with the
weight of the hour. His hand reached for his jacket when the door
creaked open again.

Raven stood there.

His breath hitched. A ripple of fear and protectiveness snapped
through him. She had already wandered once, and he'd risked far
too much helping her return unnoticed.

"Raven—" he whispered, startled. "You shouldn't be here."

Her posture was calm, composed in that unnervingly adult way of hers. Then, a small, deliberate smile, practiced, not spontaneous.

"Hello, Dr. Tenebris."

Lucien blinked, disarmed by the softness in her tone.

"It's... nice to see you," he managed.

She stepped inside, hands clasped behind her back like she'd been taught. "I'm sorry. I know you were leaving. I couldn't sleep. And I..." she hesitated, a flicker of something young breaking through, "I hoped you might be here."

Lucien exhaled, defeated by how much he didn't want her caught wandering again. He hung his jacket back on the hook.

"Wait here," he murmured, moving back to the workstation.

He reached for a couple of beakers, mixing the mild sedative blend the facility approved for "youth subjects." He adjusted the ratios, just slightly, adding a few drops of fruit extract he kept for himself. He poured the soft pink liquid into a glass and handed it to her.

"Drink this. It should help you sleep."

Raven accepted the glass with both hands and took a sip. Her eyes widened in quiet wonder.

"Wow... it's so fruity! It tastes delicious."

Lucien gave a faint, tired smile. "I tend to do better in here than in my kitchen."

She stepped closer, reaching toward him to return the glass, a small, ordinary gesture, but her hand brushed his. Skin against skin. For a moment, neither of them moved.

Then—

The world snapped.

A crack of soundless light.
A pressure behind his eyes like something tearing open.
The lab floor rippled away into black.
Raven gasped, the first truly childlike sound he'd ever heard from her.

Both of them fell—

not physically,
but into each other.

Into memory.

The glass slipped from Raven's fingers. It didn't shatter. The moment stretched too long for sound. Lucien felt her skin against his. Warm. Small. Then the warmth inverted, a cold pressure flooding up his arm, into his spine, behind his eyes.

The lab vanished.

A corridor of white light.
Boots striking tile.
A line of children standing stiff-backed,
Silent, perfectly still.
A woman's voice, clipped, sharpened:
"T-853, eyes forward."
Raven sees it, but she also feels it:
The command settling in her bones,

The stillness trained into her muscles.
Lucien feels it too.
His breath catches in his throat,
His chest seized with a discipline that isn't his.

Then –

Flicker.
A living room. Warm.
A cat curled on a faded blanket.
A younger Lucien at a kitchen table,
Sleeves pulled over his hands,
A woman yelling in the distance,
Words indistinct, tone sharp, cutting.
Raven feels the humiliation he never names.
The way he folds into himself.
The way he learned to take up less space.
Her fingers twitch in mimicry.
His shame echoes in her small shoulders.

Lucien again enters Raven's mind.

Bright lights.
A metal chair bolted to the floor.
A man in a white mask holding her wrist,
Forcing her hand to touch a stranger's skin.
Images slamming through her skull,
Hundreds, rapid-fire, unfiltered.
A scream she doesn't make aloud.
Lucien reels.
His knees buckle,
Though he isn't really standing.
His throat closes around her silent terror.
He feels what she felt:
The violation of unwanted memory,

The dizzying flood of someone else's pain,
The command afterward—
"Again."

Flicker.

Lucien,
Just a few months ago,
Standing outside Section 9 on his first day,
Hands shoved in his coat,
Looking small,
Overwhelmed,
Hopeful despite everything.
Raven sees that hope —
and it startles her.
She has never seen hope like this before.
Not this soft.

The memories overlap.

Her loneliness.
His loneliness.
Her obedience.
His avoidance.
Her training.
His masking.
Her fear of disappointing handlers.
His fear of disappointing everyone.
Her instinct to seek him out.
His instinct to protect her, without knowing why.
Their breaths sync.
Their pulses thrum together.
The floor beneath them feels no longer real.
For one suspended heartbeat—
They see each other.
Not as doctor and child.

Not as scientist and subject.
Not as stranger and stray.
But as two mirrors
Finally held up to one another
Unaware of the word,
But resonating with the truth.

A sound like tearing fabric split the air. The lab lurched back into existence.

Lucien staggered, one hand slamming against the counter to keep upright. Raven gasped and clutched her chest, knees bending as if gravity had doubled. For a moment, neither of them could breathe.

The silence between them felt too loud, too charged, the echo of what they saw still clung to their skin.

Lucien was the first to find his voice, thin, unsteady.

"Raven... what was that?"

She swallowed hard, eyes flicking up to him with a bewilderment that didn't belong on a child's face.

"I don't know," she whispered. "I've never—"

Her voice failed. She shook her head once, slow, as if trying to reset her thoughts. Lucien steadied himself against the counter, breath uneven. He forced himself to speak.

"That number you said. T-853."

He waited. She didn't correct him.

"That... prefix. 'T.' It's used for the guards. I learned that when I started here.”

He wet his lips. “Their folder called them Tapaha. Do you know what that means?”

Raven looked down at her small hands, flexing them once as if remembering the feel of the memory-cross.

“I know I’m... different,” she said quietly. “I know I see things when I touch people. Things that already happened. Things that hurt.” Her fingers curled inward. “They train us to do that.”

Lucien felt his pulse spike at *train us.*

He forced himself to exhale, gentle. “What happened just now?” he asked softly. “When you touched me?”

Raven’s brows knit. Her voice dropped to a trembling hush.

“That part is strange,” she admitted. “I saw *your* memories.” She pauses. “But at the same time... you saw mine.”

She lifted her eyes, dark and earnest.

“That’s never happened before.”

Lucien’s breath caught. Their confusion mirrored each other perfectly, two people circling the edges of a truth neither of them had a name for.

A harsh burst of static.

“Subject T-853 missing. Repeat: T-853 missing. Initiate containment sweep.”

Boots thundered down the hallway.

Lucien spun, panic rising like bile.
He pointed frantically toward the service door he'd used before.

"Raven—over here! Quick!"

She darted toward it, small and silent, slipping through just as he hit the manual override.

The panel sealed behind her.

Lucien grabbed his jacket, heart in his throat, and forced himself out of the lab, casual, hurried but not running, trying not to draw eyes. By the time he reached his car, his hands were shaking so violently he could barely get the key into the ignition.

Raven moved quickly through the dim corridor, heading toward the barracks—

—but a tall white figure stepped from the shadows, blocking her path.

A T-Regime guard. White armor. White gloves. Blank mask. Expressionless, yet somehow staring straight through her. His distorted mechanical voice filled the space.

"T-853. Unauthorized roaming detected."

Raven froze.

"Please..." she whispered, voice cracking. "Please don't take me to Father."

The guard seized her by the inside of her elbow, clinical, not cruel, but absolute. Raven flinched, her feet skidding on the tile as he turned her sharply. He marched her down the hall. Past the barracks. Past the training rooms. Past the place she expected punishment, toward the office of the Secretary of Defense.

Cassian Drehl.

The door slid open with a soft pneumatic sigh. Warm lamplight spilled out. A silhouette waited inside. The guard pushed Raven forward.

"Subject retrieved," he announced.

Drehl's voice, smooth, composed, unreadable, answered from the shadows:

"Bring her to me."

XI

Lucien swung the door open to the house. Yusra, having finished her semester and quietly avoiding the public eye, sat curled on the couch with a half-finished blanket pooled at her side. The cold weather had finally settled in; a mug of mint tea steamed on the coffee table. Her knitting needles paused mid-row as she looked up at him, brow furrowed.

"Lucien... you look like you've seen a ghost. What's wrong?"

He shook his head, already pacing, fingers clawing for loose seams at the cuffs of his sweater. His eyes darted from wall to wall, hunting for something he couldn't name.

Yusra rose slowly, stepping into his path, one hand pressing to her own chest.

"Lucien. Remember..."

She inhaled. Exhaled. He mirrored her automatically, a reflex built from months of her grounding him through spirals.

When his shoulders finally dropped a fraction, she motioned toward his armchair. He sank into it, closing his eyes, tipping his head back against the cushion. Another breath in. Another out. Just one more. When he opened his eyes, they flicked straight to his fidgeting fingers.

Mercury, sensing everything before anyone spoke it aloud, hopped into his lap and curled there, purring with a soft, steady insistence. The vibration anchored him more than he expected.

Lucien swallowed, voice tiny.

"Raven…"

Yusra blinked. "Raven? The girl you met at the lab?"

He froze. Then he turned toward her, *truly* turned, locking onto her gaze with an intensity she'd never seen from him. It stole her breath more than it frightened her. It was the first time she had really seen his eyes up close: those strange, shifting pools of lily-pad green rimmed with warm gold, lit now by the soft lamps around the room. Something in them trembled.

"You told me to tell you everything about that word," he whispered.

"'Tapaha'?"

"Yes."

"Have you found out something new?"

Lucien pauses, eyes darting back to his hands, as he wrings them raw.

"Our hands touched. It was like the world split. All of a sudden, I'm seeing flashes of the things she's experienced, this extremely militant training, her memories of touching people and being flooded by *their* memories. Even stranger, I could feel her seeing my memories back."

Yusra's eyes widen. The story seems wild, but she knows with Lucien, he would never lie to her.

"You saw each other's memories? How is that possible?"

"I asked her after about what they named her, T-853, about being categorized as that word – 'Tapaha.' She told me that's what happens, that they touch people, and can witness that person's most intimate moments." He pauses to chew his nails.

"That is bizarre! It's no wonder the government could be keeping this a secret. What exactly are they up to?"

"It gets stranger." He inhales. Exhales. Lucien's voice thinned. "She said no one before me ever saw her memories back."

Yusra stared at him, knitting forgotten, her breath pausing mid-chest.

"Lucien... that isn't... normal. People don't just exchange memories."

"I know." His fingers trembled as he clutched Mercury a little tighter. "But she reacted like she *felt* something. Like she was inside my mind. She kept asking what I was."

Yusra moved closer, lowering herself onto the edge of the coffee table so she could really see him.

"What did *you* feel? Not what you saw — *you*. What was happening inside you when it happened?"

Lucien pressed a hand to his forehead, closing his eyes, reliving the moment in real time as Yusra witnessed.

"It was like something pulled forward inside me. Like a pressure in my palms. Heat. Then everything opened all at once. Her memories, mine... overlapping. Tangled. The worst part?" His voice cracked. "It didn't feel impossible. It felt... familiar. Like something I should have understood."

Yusra's pulse quickened at that. Familiar did not mean accidental. Familiar meant intrinsic. She steadied her voice.

"Has this ever happened to you before?"

"Nothing like this, although..."

Yusra's eyes grow wider. She mutters.

"Although what?"

"It's so infrequent. I simply don't touch people, but in these rare instances when a person has made contact with my skin, there may be strange musings. Voices I don't recognize, smells that shouldn't be there, visions. I don't do much with that. I just try to avoid touching people altogether. Touch is always far too loud."

A faint tremor threaded through her ribs, one she refused to let reach her voice.

"Lucien... this isn't you doing something wrong. This is something happening to you — something that was already there."

He blinked, shaken.

"So you think something's wrong with me."

"No." Her answer was immediate. "I think something about you doesn't match what that lab believes about people like her. That means we need to understand it before anyone else notices."

Lucien looked down at Mercury, petting him slowly, grounding himself.

"So what do I do?"

"For now?" Yusra leaned in, voice low, deliberate. "You tell me everything you remember. Every flicker, every sensation. Anything she said. Anything you felt. All of it."

He nodded, swallowing hard.

"And..." she added carefully, "I think at some point, I need to see that place."

Lucien's head snapped up. "Yusra, no. You can't just walk into my lab. There are guards. Keycards. Surveillance. It's not a place you sneak into."

"I'm aware."

Her voice didn't waver, though concern flickered behind her eyes.

"But this, whatever happened to you, it's connected to that building. To their research. I can't help you if I'm blind to what you're walking into every day."

Lucien looked at her, terrified, not of her plan, but that she even considered risking herself for him.

"You'd really do that? For me?"

Yusra gave him a soft, aching smile.

"For you? For the truth? Lucien… of course I would."

As he began recounting the memory in halting, trembling detail, Yusra listened with growing unease. Whatever this "Tapaha" word meant, it was no longer an abstract curiosity.

It was waking up inside the person she cared for most.

Raven sat in the chair before Drehl's desk, posture flawless despite her plaid pajamas, hands folded as if awaiting judgment. Her eyes stayed downcast.

"Father, I—"

Drehl rose from his desk without acknowledging her voice. He moved toward the bookcase with slow, predatory calm, the soft scrape of his shoes the only sound.

"T-853," he said, his back still turned, "you know what happens when you break protocol."

Raven's breath shook. "Please, Father, it was Dr. Tenebris I went to see."

Drehl paused, fingertips resting on the spine of a leather-bound volume. He did not look at her.

"The scientist," he repeated, tone flat. "Why in God's name were you with the scientist?"

"I... don't know. He's—" She hesitated, knowing how thin the ice beneath her was. "He's interesting."

That was when Drehl turned. Not with anger. Not yet. Only with the slow, deliberate precision of a man inspecting a fracture in something expensive he owns.

"Interesting enough to violate a direct order?"

Raven swallowed, her spine rigid, her voice barely above a whisper.

"Father, something happened in that lab."

A spark flickered in Drehl's eyes, irritation, but also something sharper.

"Explain."

Raven hesitated. She had never done this, defied him, asked him to listen rather than obey. "When we touched hands, I saw his memories. I saw *him*."

"You were built for that," Drehl snapped. "Observation is your assignment."

"No." Raven shook her head quickly, fearful of seeming defiant. "No, Father. He saw *mine*."

The air in the room shifted. Drehl moved closer, each step heavy with new calculation.

"What did you say?"

Raven forced herself not to shrink. "He saw my memories. Not just flashes. He stepped into them. No one has ever done that before."

Drehl stared at her as if seeing her for the first time.

"And he knew?" he asked.

"Yes."

Drehl let out a slow breath, not quite disbelief, but more like revelation.

"My God," he murmured. "A reciprocal interface."

Raven nodded quickly. "He didn't mean to. He didn't even know what he was. I think it frightened him."

"Oh, T-853..." Drehl's voice softened in a way that wasn't kind, merely intimate, ownership masquerading as affection. "Do you understand what this means?"

Raven shook her head.

Drehl's hand came down on her shoulder, heavy, approving. "This is not a breach. This is an opportunity."

Her eyes darted up, startled.

"Father?"

"Your designation no longer reflects your usefulness," he said, releasing her. "You've outgrown it." He circled back toward his desk with newfound energy. "The public will need a name for you... something respectable. Something that conceals what you are while elevating who you will become."

He flipped open a drawer and pulled out a folder already prepared, prepared long before she ever earned it.

"Alenya Creed," he said, almost smiling. "That will be your identity moving forward. A promising young representative. Clean. Loyal. Untouchable."

Raven blinked. "Am I... am I not being punished?"

"No, child," Drehl said, pleased in a way that chilled her bones. "You are being positioned. You are now T-Regime, but more importantly, our secret weapon."

He clasped his hands behind his back, eyes gleaming.

"If the scientist can access memories as you do, he is not merely a scientist. He is a breach in the wall we have built. And you—" He tilted his head, examining her. "You will be the bridge."

Raven sat very still.

Her training had not prepared her for this: the moment obedience turned into purpose. Purpose tasted more dangerous than punishment ever had.

Somewhere far from that office, the man who unwittingly awakened that purpose was shaking in his living room, unaware that a new name had already begun to reshape his fate.

XII

Tonight would be the night.

They had said it aloud only once, their voices barely above a whisper in the dim light of their home. After that, the plan existed only in exchanged looks, quiet movements, and the mutual understanding that something inside both of them had already crossed a threshold. The city outside their windows felt brittle and waiting, as if it knew what they were about to do.

Yusra pressed her palm against her thigh, steadying the tremor beneath her skin. Lucien didn't look at her directly; if he did, something in him might break. Instead, he watched the way her breath fogged the cold air, the way her shoulders lifted and lowered as she braced herself.

"Once we're in," he whispered, "stay close, but don't touch me. And don't speak unless you have to."

"I know," she murmured.

The National Guard convoys rumbled somewhere far off, the sound rolling over the city like distant thunder. Vaughn's latest speech echoed faintly from a billboard screen, distorted by wind. The regime's presence was everywhere now, in every shadow.

"Let's go," Lucien said.

The first lie came at the gate.

"I left my access card inside," he told the night guard, voice flattened by exhaustion he didn't have to fake. "I need to rerun the T-series assays before morning."

He kept his gaze fixed, his mind begging his face not to give him away. He felt like every muscle in his face could betray him, but for Yusra, he held steady. The guard barely blinked. His eyes were dull with fatigue, worn by too many shifts, too much vigilance, too little sleep in a nation turning in on itself.

He scanned Lucien's badge. The light blinked green.

Lucien slipped through. Yusra waited until his body blocked the guard's peripheral view, then swept to the fence's base and pulled his satchel through the small gap they had scouted earlier.

He didn't look. He didn't have to.

They separated, then reconvened once he had opened the service hallway door from the inside.

Section 9's service corridor was cold, the air smelling of disinfectant and metal. The flickering fluorescent light cast broken shadows across the walls.

"This way," Lucien whispered. "We can reach my lab through the back corridor."

Yusra nodded and followed him silently.

He led with a strange certainty. Not memory. At least not his own. It felt more like instinct, or something deeper than instinct. The walls felt familiar under his fingertips, though he had never walked this route. Not awake, anyway.

They passed a storage alcove, then another. The air changed subtly, colder, thinner, the hallway itself holding its breath. Pipes overhead vibrated in irregular pulses, each mechanical shudder echoing faintly through the metal lattice.

Yusra slowed.

"Lucien..." she whispered.

He turned slightly, not enough to touch her, just enough to show he was listening.

"It feels like someone is down here."

He swallowed. "There shouldn't be. This wing is usually empty at night."

"Usually," she echoed, her voice thin. "I don't like that word in a place like this."

They slipped into a narrow side room tucked behind the main corridor, a cold, humming space lit by a single bluish lamp. A row of refrigeration units lined the wall. In the center, a metal prep table held trays of labeled vials awaiting processing.

Yusra leaned closer, squinting.

Series T — Intake Pending
Series B — Stabilized
Series J — Observation Required

Her eyebrows knit. "What do these letters mean?"

Lucien shifted uneasily. "Just categories. Project groupings. I don't work with these directly."

"Categories of what?"

"I... don't know."

"Seems an awful lot like they're experimenting on people."

"They use volunteers."
"I don't know, Lucien..."

A faint mechanical click sounded in the vents above them. They both froze. After a tense moment, Lucien motioned toward the far door.

"Come on. My lab is through here."

A low clank echoed from somewhere deep in the ventilation system. Not footsteps. Worse in a way. Mechanical. Intentional. The building shifted its weight. Yusra pressed close to the wall, her eyes scanning every corner, every shadow.

"Do they have cameras in this hallway?"

"I have no idea," Lucien admitted. "I only ever go where they escort me."

"That doesn't reassure me."

He didn't respond. Nothing here reassured him either. At the next intersection, Lucien paused, as if trying to recall a map that had never been taught to him. The air shifted again, bringing with it a faint chemical scent, metallic and sweet. Yusra's expression tightened.

"What is that?" she murmured.

He shook his head. "I—I don't know. Something they use in another department."

Yusra's eyes flicked upward. "It smells like something burned."

Lucien stiffened. "I've smelled that before. I don't know what it is. They never tell me."

She stared at him. "Do you think it's normal?"

"I don't know what 'normal' is in this place," he whispered.

Yusra exhaled shakily. Lucien motioned for her to follow, and they turned down the left corridor, the one that tugged at something deep in him. As they moved, the hum of Section 9 seemed to grow more deliberate, more alive, the walls listening.

A faint click sounded behind them. Yusra froze.

Lucien's breath hitched. "Probably just pressure release."

"You keep saying probably," she whispered.

He almost smiled, a tight, pained expression. "It's the only comfort I can offer."

They reached the restricted-access panel. Lucien lifted his badge, hand trembling slightly, whether from fear or instinctive dread, he didn't know.

"Are you sure?" Yusra whispered.

"No," he said honestly. "But we're out of options."

The reader scanned. A beat too long. Then it clicked green. The lock disengaged with a soft metallic sigh. Lucien pushed the door open.

The space felt different with Yusra inside it. Smaller somehow, more exposed.

The room was dim, lit only by the standby glow of screens and the faint pulse of refrigerated units. His workstation, usually cluttered with half-finished notes, labeled vials, and printed data sheets, now looked exposed, incriminating, the room waiting for someone else's eyes to give it meaning.

Yusra stepped forward slowly, taking in everything. The charts. The sample racks. The coded labels. The cold neatness of it all.

"Is this where you work every day?" she whispered.

Lucien hesitated. "Yes."

She approached a tray of vials. The red fluid inside each glinted faintly under the monitors' glow. Labels marked with Series T, B, and J lined the tray, identical to the ones they'd seen in storage, but here, they were organized by analysis status.

Yusra hovered her hands above a stack of intake logs beside the tray.

"Can I look?"

He nodded stiffly. She sifted through them, careful not to smudge or disturb anything. Names were redacted. Entire lines were blacked out. On several pages, faint, incomplete, half-erased by the technician's sloppy censoring, the intake dates still showed a single digit before the blackout.

Her brows lifted, just slightly, catching something the eye wasn't meant to register.

13 / –– / 52
13 / –– / 51
13 / –– / ––

Yusra froze.

"...Lucien."

He turned toward her sharply.

"These dates."
She tapped the page gently.

"They're redacted, but the day wasn't scrubbed out. Every intake I can see was logged on the thirteenth."

He blinked, confused. "That's... probably just when they process transfers. An administrative cycle."

"You really believe that?" she whispered.

He didn't answer. She laid more sheets side by side. The same pattern: the number 13, over and over, half-covered but unmistakable.

"It's too consistent to be coincidence," she said.

"It's too little information to mean anything," he insisted.

Her voice softened, but the softness cut deeper.

"That's what terrifies me, Luci. You keep saying you don't know enough to question anything."

He swallowed hard. She moved to his workstation monitor, tapping gently at the lines of data.

"These aren't normal study logs. These are profiles. Intake timestamps. Sedation patterns. Trauma indexing. All of it stripped of context. You're studying aftermaths without seeing any cause."

"That's how they trained me to work," he said quietly.

"That's how they blinded you."

He flinched. She looked at the room again, at the cold precision of it, the mechanical heartbeat of a place built not for healing but for containment.

"This is not research," she whispered. "This is record-keeping for something they're not letting you see."

She opened her mouth to say more—

CRACKLE

A sharp noise split the air overhead. Both of them stiffened. The ceiling speaker hissed, then a voice came through, metallic and flat:

"Sub-level personnel, status verification required. Sweep in progress. All staff confirm station presence immediately."

Lucien's blood ran cold.

"They're checking the wings," he whispered. "We need to go. Now."

"How do we get out?"

He pointed toward the back access door he'd never consciously used, but which tugged at him now like a memory not his own.

"This way."

Yusra didn't hesitate. They moved quickly through the back corridor, Lucien navigating instinctively. No touch. No sound but their footsteps. No certainty. Boots echoed faintly above them, guards sweeping the upper floors. Lucien quickened his pace, gesturing sharply for Yusra to follow. They reached a narrow, dim hallway lit by a single green EXIT sign.

The footsteps grew louder. He pushed against the EXIT bar. For a moment, it didn't move.

Then it gave.

Cold night air rushed in, sharp and welcome. They climbed the external stairwell to a gravel strip between two wings. The building loomed over them, silent and waiting. Boots clattered on the metal stairs below. Voices murmured. Radios crackled.

Then, gradually, the sounds drifted away.

"That was almost us," Yusra whispered.

"It wasn't," Lucien said, though his voice trembled. "We're fine."

"For now."

They parted ways according to plan. Lucien exited through the employee checkpoint, signing out under the bored eye of the night guard. Yusra disappeared into the darkened streets and waited beneath the dead neon of a laundromat sign. When he reached her, she didn't move.

"You saw enough," she said.

Lucien shook his head. "I saw incomplete records. Redacted data. Nothing... definitive."

"That's what they count on." Her voice was quiet, almost tender in its sadness. "They bury the truth under so much nothing that you stop believing there's something underneath."

He looked away.

"If I quit," he said, "they'll notice. People don't just leave Section 9."

"You staying won't keep you safe," she whispered. "It will make you useful."

The words lanced him. She stepped closer.

"When you're ready to leave," she said, "I'll help you, but I won't pretend any of this is fine."

He swallowed. "Go home. Lock the door."

She studied him with an ache too deep for words.

"Just make sure you come back."

She disappeared into the dark.

Lucien stood alone beneath the buzzing neon, feeling the cold sink into his bones. Behind his eyes, the faint shape of the number 13 flickered, meaningless and intrusive.

It meant nothing yet, but unsettled him in a way he couldn't explain. Something inside him had cracked. Cracks, once made, only deepen.

XIII

Tonight should have felt louder. For months, advisors warned him that the first night of the cleansing would be chaos: screaming cities, burning barricades, endless noise.

The sound in Vaughn's private chamber, however, was gentle.

On the wall of screens before him, the nation flickered like a constellation breaking apart. Distant fires pulsed along the coasts, sharp red blooms where resistance cells were being "retrieved." Streets seethed with floodlights and armored convoys, but the noise of it, the real human noise, arrived muted through the glass.

He preferred it that way.

He watched the National Guard sweep through Seattle's northern district, a clean formation cutting through the dark. People ran. People fell. People were loaded into vans whose windows had long been painted over. Even through the feed's static, he could see the moment crowds realized the rules had changed. They always knew, eventually.

A slow breath slipped from his chest, warm and steady.

Order, he thought. *At last.*

The generals begged him to delay. They wanted more time, more logistics, more assurances. Vaughn knew that too much time was where a nation rotted. Delay was the language of the coward, the bureaucrat, the weak-willed. Purification required conviction. Tonight, the country would remember what conviction looked like.

He stepped closer to the screen showing Boston. A fire raged through the old financial district, not from his forces, but from the crowds themselves. A warehouse exploded moments before; now a column of flame tore upward like a furious sunrise. People surged around it, screaming, fleeing, fighting. The chaos delighted him in a quiet, private way.

Fire was a revelation. It revealed who people truly were.

Another feed appeared: Chicago. Armored vehicles rolled through snow-choked streets, headlights cutting bright spears across the darkness. Soldiers dragged a line of protestors into a transport truck. One woman kicked, another wept, another seemed to be praying. Vaughn watched them dispassionately, the way he would observe insects crossing a countertop.

It was not cruelty. It was distance. They were necessary parts of a necessary night.

He touched his fingertips to the screen, following the movement of a convoy disappearing beneath an overpass. There had been chatter earlier in the year, nervous advisors wondering how the public abductions would be received. Vaughn had been unbothered. The fear in people's faces was proof of awakening. Fear was clarity. Fear stripped away the indulgent illusions of freedom and returned them to truth.

The enemy within had grown bold these past years. Root rot at the center of the nation's heartwood. If this war was brutal, it was because the infection was deep. He would carve until the tree stood clean.

Another window opened: Richmond. A plume of white smoke rose from a government complex, obscuring figures collapsing against the pavement. No one explained the source. He didn't ask. Every operation tonight was meant to be decisive. No surgical cuts. No hesitant gestures. The nation could only be reborn through overwhelming force.

He leaned back in his chair, letting his eyes drift across the feeds. It reminded him of the nights he used to sit at his grandfather's knee, listening to the old man speak of biblical judgment, of nations that fell because they refused to purify themselves. He remembered those stories now, the thunderous cadence of them, the simplicity of their moral lines. A nation either cleansed itself or it perished.

There was no third path.

A small smile ghosted across Vaughn's lips. Somewhere below the complex, in rooms he rarely visited, ministers and officers were cataloguing the night's results. How many taken. How many silenced. How many pockets of resistance still flared like bone fragments refusing to dissolve. This phase would last days, maybe hours if the Guard executed well. Vaughn knew none of those details personally. He didn't need to.

He concerned himself only with the vision. The purity. The shape of the world he was carving into being.

A new alert chimed softly. Drone footage began streaming from the outskirts of Atlanta. Vaughn's eyes sharpened. Columns of civilians were being herded across an empty freeway, thousands of them, a dark river of bodies moving under armed escort. Some stumbled. Some tried to break away and were met with swift correction. Most simply walked.

He felt something inside him settle. A warmth. A certainty. This was what he had promised the nation. This was what he had warned them would come. A country too fractured to save would be cleansed instead. A country cleansed through obedience.

Aides would later ask him to address the public at dawn. He already knew what he would say. He wouldn't speak of bombings or captures or the frantic violence of the night. He would speak of renewal. Of unity. Of the courage required to cut away decay so that something unbroken could grow.

He would tell them they were safe. He would tell them he was saving them. He would believe it.

On the wall of screens, the fire in Boston shifted color, from orange to a pale, radiant white. For a moment, the district looked almost washed clean. Vaughn watched it burn, and his voice, low and reverent, filled the empty room:

"Good."

He folded his hands behind his back, chin lifting slightly as the feeds cycled through new scenes, new cities, new flames, new fractures forming exactly where he had always expected them.

The war had not begun tonight. The war had always been here. Tonight was simply the first night the nation finally admitted it.

By morning, they would understand that he had been right all along.

XIV

In Section 9, the war outside changed nothing.

The facility did not shake with the explosions in the cities above it; no alarms blared when martial law took hold. The hallways remained sterile. The routines continued. The only sign that anything beyond their walls had shifted was the sudden, quiet pressure in the air, supervisors speaking in clipped tones, guards doubling patrols, locked doors staying locked a little longer.

Lucien noticed it only in the margins: more escorts in the corridors, fewer briefings, and a silence beneath everything that hadn't been there before.

Lucien did not intend to break protocol. He only wanted to confirm the numbers. He had been running chromosomal stability checks on a Redline sample all morning, cross-referencing it with the expected genomic patterns he was taught in onboarding: adult volunteers, trauma-therapy candidates, severity tiers one through five; however, the strands on his terminal didn't match adult physiology. They matched juvenile markers.

Repeatedly.

He blinked hard, recalibrated the scanner, and ran the test again. Still juvenile. Still consistent. Still impossible.

A thin, panicked hum began in his throat, an involuntary stim rising with every repeated scan. His breath hitched. His fingers trembled against the keyboard.

This was a child's blood, and not just any child. A Bhuvaha child.

He had seen the classification term only once during onboarding, redacted in three separate places. The sanitized definition had been something vague:

"Subjects with intense neural memory signatures requiring specialized protocols."

He had assumed the Bhuvaha were a small group of volunteers. Children were never mentioned. Not once.

His chest tightened, breath stuttering. He had to know. He had to see.

Before he could talk himself out of it, he ripped off his gloves, grabbed his badge, and stumbled toward the elevator, the one marked Authorized Personnel Only. He had never gone to the upper restricted level alone. T-Regime escorts had always flanked him in their immaculate white suits, rifles held vertical against their chests, blank masks revealing nothing. They walked him where he was allowed to go and nowhere else.

Today, no one was waiting. The elevator doors slid open with a soft chime. Cold air rushed in. He stepped out.

The hallway stretched ahead in a sterile line, white walls, reinforced doors, observation windows at intervals. The quiet was wrong, thick, padded, heavy. He listened for the familiar cadence of bootsteps, the clipped murmur of guards, anything.

Nothing.

His palms dampened. He wiped them against his coat and moved forward.

The first window stopped him.

He hadn't known about this room. No one had mentioned a central holding quadrant. The space beyond the glass yawned wide, a cavern segmented by thick partitions, each section holding prisoners chained to floor bolts.

Bhuvaha.

He knew it instinctively. He didn't need the small, red-stamped classification in the corner of the monitor to confirm it. Men. Women. Teenagers. All separated. All shackled. Ankles ringed with metal, wrists bound behind their backs or anchored to wall loops. No one was allowed close enough to touch anyone else.

Many stared at nothing, hollow-eyed, bodies thinned by malnutrition. Some rocked faintly, lips moving with unheard words, echoes of memories they could no longer keep contained. One woman's shoulders shook in silent sobs; another lay curled on her side, eyes open, unseeing.

Lucien's stomach knotted. He pressed his hand to the glass, as if that might steady the tremor that had started in his arm. The onboarding language rang in his ears again, mockingly benign:

"Some subjects require extended observation between sessions as part of their stabilization protocol."

Observation? Fuck no. This was cattle herding. He forced himself to move on, each step heavier than the last.

The next window was worse.

Inside, the room was smaller, more focused. Rows of metal beds lined each wall, each holding a child. Eight. Ten. Twelve years old. Bhuvaha, every one of them. Their wrists and ankles were bound with padded restraints. Electrodes clung to their temples and along their spines. Clear tubing snaked from ports at the base of their skulls into collection cylinders mounted on steel brackets. Several cylinders already glowed with that sickening, familiar iridescence.

Redline. Not filtered. Not refined.

Raw.

A Janaha in all black moved between the beds, mask gleaming under the overhead lights. His gloved hand hovered over a child's head, fingers pressing, not gently, against a tear-streaked cheek. The boy's body arched, a convulsion ripping through him as his memories were stripped away molecule by molecule.

The collection cylinder at his bedside brightened.

Lucien's knees went weak. He caught himself on the wall, fingers scraping against cold metal. He wanted to look away. He couldn't.

The Janaha withdrew his hand. The boy sagged, limp against the restraints, chest rising in thin, ragged breaths. Another technician checked a panel, nodded, and adjusted a dial.

A notation blinked on a nearby monitor:
C-03 | Cycle 3 | Yield: Optimal

Lucien slapped a hand over his mouth. A choked sound escaped anyway. Volunteers?

He had read those words a hundred times in the project briefings.

"All Section 9 participants are vetted and consented, contributing voluntarily to groundbreaking trauma research."

Volunteers didn't look like this. Didn't scream like this. Didn't have their childhood poured into tubes so it could be inhaled in elite lounges.

His chest burned. His breath came high and fast, skimming the top of his lungs. He stumbled backward, nearly tripping over his own feet as he forced himself away from the window.

One more, he thought, without knowing why. Just one more.

The last window at the end of the corridor showed a different kind of room. Smaller. Too bright.

Solitary.

He recognized it now but from whispers that slipped between the lines of his cleared documents. High-risk subjects. Individual evaluation. Special observation chamber. There were no beds in this room. No rows. No partitions.

Just one pair of restraints descending from the ceiling. One drain set into the tile floor. One table with gleaming instruments laid out in perfect symmetry.

The far wall was all glass, but not like the viewing pane Lucien stood behind. This glass was dark from this side.

One-way.

Beyond it, offset by reflections, he could see the suggestion of movement: shadows of seated figures, the gentle lift of a drink, the tilt of a masked head. Softer light. Upholstery. The faint outline of what might have been a bar.

The Visitation lounge.

He had heard the term before. High-clearance debriefing. Donor observation. Stakeholder demonstrations. Euphemisms that sounded clinical on paper. Seeing it made his skin crawl.

The door to the solitary chamber opened. A single Bhuvaha prisoner was led inside by two white-suited T-Regime officers. Their masks were as blank as ever, rifles slung over their shoulders, boots nearly silent on the tile. The prisoner's wrists were already bruised where restraints had cut into them. Their steps faltered at the sight of the room. Lucien watched the recognition wash over their face with horrible clarity. They knew what this room meant.

The guards hoisted the prisoner's arms up into the ceiling cuffs. Metal clinked against metal as the restraints locked. One of the officers adjusted the height, forcing the prisoner onto the balls of their feet, body stretched at an impossible angle.

Lucien's fingers dug into the edge of the window frame. From the lounge, a tall figure stepped into view behind the dark glass. Black suit. Obsidian mask. Hands clasped behind his back. Even through the distortion, Lucien recognized that sleek blonde hair immediately.

Senator Elias Crane.

The Janaha inclined his head once. A signal. One of the guards struck the prisoner across the ribs with a baton. The sound didn't travel through the soundproof glass, but Lucien felt it, the way the prisoner's body jerked, the way their mouth opened on a silent cry.

Another strike. Another. A slow, methodical rhythm.

Lucien's vision narrowed. The corners of his sight pulsed with black. He realized dimly that he had stopped breathing somewhere between strikes three and four. The onboarding line came back again, warped and obscene now:

"Solitary sessions provide a controlled environment for intensive cognitive work."

His knees hit the floor. A broken sound tore out of him, half-sob, half-animal. His hands shook so hard he had to brace them against the tile. He had walked this hallway before, escorted swiftly past sealed doors, white rifles brushing his peripheral vision. He had seen children in stiff military uniforms once, where he first saw Alenya, standing in a line near a training room, eyes forward, gloved hands locked behind their backs. He had allowed himself to believe it was a program. A study. Something clean.

He couldn't believe that anymore. Not after this. Not after the children in the extraction room. Not after the prisoners in chains. Not after Crane.

The world tilted. Someone grabbed his shoulder. He flinched violently, a strangled noise ripping from his throat as he twisted around. A T-Regime officer loomed over him, white suit, white gloves, white blank mask. The rifle slung over his chest gleamed under the corridor light.

"Dr. Tenebris," the officer said, voice muffled and perfectly even. "You are not authorized for this sector."

Lucien opened his mouth. No words came. His tongue felt thick, throat locked in that familiar, hateful vise of mutism. The officer's grip tightened just slightly.

"You must return to your lab."

Lucien's breathing sped up, fast and shallow. His stims fired in wild, disjointed bursts, hands flexing, shoulders jerking, heel tapping against the floor.

"I..." He forced the sound out. "I—can't."

"Repeat your last statement," the officer said.

Lucien's chest clenched.

"I can't," he choked. "I can't— I won't— I—"

The words scraped out of him raw, building on each other until they broke free in a single, hoarse shout.

"I QUIT!"

The hallway swallowed the sound, but it echoed in his bones. The officer didn't move. Lucien lurched to his feet, swaying.

"Do you hear me?" he demanded, voice cracking. "I'm done. I'm not— I'm not part of this. I quit."

For a long, terrible moment, the white mask simply stared at him.

Then, calmly, the officer tapped the comm at his collar.

"Control, this is Sector Three. Dr. Lucien Tenebris has breached restricted corridors and expressed intent to abandon his assignment. Flag as compromised. Retrieval requested."

The word retrieval landed like a physical blow. Lucien's heart slammed against his ribs. He ran.

He didn't remember choosing a direction. His body just moved, bolting down the corridor, back toward the elevator, boots slipping slightly on the polished floor. He jabbed the call button. The doors slid open with excruciating slowness. He stumbled inside, slammed his palm against the panel, and watched the restricted floor disappear as the elevator began its descent. His reflection stared back at him in the metal: wide eyes, ashen skin, a smear of something. He wasn't sure if it was dust or the beginning of a nosebleed beneath one nostril.

He'd seen too much. He'd finally seen what Section 9 really was. In some distant, rational corner of his mind that hadn't yet shattered, he knew:

They were never going to let him walk away.

XV

The front door slammed so hard the frame rattled.

Lucien stumbled inside, shoulders hunched, fingers buried in his hair as if trying to physically hold his mind together. He paced the length of the living room in sharp, panicked strides, indiscernible sounds spilling from his mouth, half-breaths, half-syllables, nothing like language.

Yusra looked up from the dining table, startled.
She'd never seen him like this.

"Lucien?" she whispered. "What's wrong?"

His mouth opened, but only fragments broke free, small, strangled words punched through a wall of panic.

"Children—"
"Extraction—"
"Wrong—wrong—wrong—"
"Can't—can't—can't—"

His hands shook violently. His knees buckled. His breath hitched into shallow, frantic gasps. Yusra was already moving. She reached him carefully, placing her hands on his shoulders to steady and ground him.

"Lucien," she said gently, "look at me. Breathe with me, okay?"

She inhaled slowly, visibly. Exhaled just as slow. Lucien tried to mimic her, but the air caught in his throat. His chest stuttered. He shook his head in a sharp, distressed jerk, eyes wide and unfocused.

"I—I quit," he choked out suddenly, the words bursting out like they'd torn their way free. "I quit—I can't—I can't—"

He backed into the couch and collapsed onto it, hands gripping the cushions as if the fabric was the only solid thing left. He didn't realize he was trembling until the couch cushions vibrated under his hands. Yusra sat closer than usual. Close, but still leaving him space to breathe. Her expression carried that rare mixture he had learned to dread: grief wrapped in determination.

"Lucien," she murmured, "something happened."

He squeezed his eyes shut. His breath came in small, broken pulls. His hands hovered near his temples, stimming in desperate, tight bursts. Yusra waited. She knew better than to push speech. When he finally managed to force out words, they came in shattered fragments.

"Children... strapped... crying..."
"Machines—"

"They— they take—"
"I didn't know— I didn't know—"

His voice cracked into a sound that wasn't quite a sob, wasn't quite a breath. Yusra's face softened. Her hands stayed visible, not touching him unless he reached first. She exhaled once, steadying herself.

"Lucien... look at me."

He lifted his eyes, raw, frantic, drowning.

"You're not losing your mind," she whispered. "You're feeling something that isn't yours."

She waited, watching the confusion shift into fear.

"You're Tapaha," she continued gently. "You've been slipping. Tiny echoes when people touch you. Flinches when someone walks into the room with grief on them. Lucien... you aren't imagining it."

Lucien swallowed, throat tight, unable to process.

"You know what you are," she said. "Even if you don't want to. I know you do."

His head shook weakly.

"No."

"Yes," she said softly.

She extended her forearm, not to force, but to offer.

"Lucien," she whispered, "I think you know that I know. I need you to trust me. Let me show you what you're feeling. Let me help you understand what you are... before they do."

He stared at her skin like it was a cliff's edge.

"Do you consent?" she asked.

He nodded once and touched her.

The room dissolved.
 Light fractured.

He stood,
Not as Yusra now,
But as Yusra then—
 Twenty-seven years old,
Exhausted, brilliant,
Still clinging to the final months of her graduate work
At the Islamic University of Gaza.
Lectures interrupted by airstrikes.
Friends texting "Are you alive?"
Instead of "Good luck on the exam."
He felt her sprinting down cracked university corridors
As the campus shook,
Carrying her laptop to the basement because she refused to lose her
thesis draft—
Again.
He felt the panic of counting which friends
Hadn't answered messages.
The guilt of reading names on casualty lists
And looking for someone she loved.
The moment she found them.
He felt her nightmares:
Bodies under concrete slabs,
the stink of dust and smoke,
the metallic taste of fear that slid down her throat and never fully

left.
Border crossings.
Hours of interrogations.
The U.S. visa officer asking her,
Politely, almost casually,
If she intended to "bring any political unrest" with her.
Landing in America:
People debating the war on cable news like it was a sport.
Classmates boycotting her lectures because they "didn't want to feel guilty."
Professors praising her "resilience" instead of her research.
The loneliness of watching the destruction of her home
through livestreams while eating microwaved dinners
in a quiet apartment no one else entered.
She had survived, but survival felt like betrayal.
She was alive, but every day she wondered if she should be.

All of it slammed into Lucien at once: her grief, her terror, her exhaustion, her faith, her anger, her relentless will to keep learning in a world that kept tearing books out of her hands.

Then the memory broke.

Lucien collapsed forward, hands shaking, lungs unable to decide between inhaling or sobbing. He curled in on himself, knees pulled tight, as if trying to hold the memories inside long enough to process them before they shattered him.

"Lucien," she murmured.

She reached toward him, then paused, waiting, offering. To her astonishment, he moved first. He leaned into her, arms wrapping around her in a desperate, unstudied motion. A hug, clumsy, terrified, but real. His forehead pressed into her shoulder, breath ragged against her collarbone. She pulled him closer, holding him like someone who understood the cost of touch.

"I'm here," she whispered. "I'm right here."

He didn't answer, but he didn't let go. Not for a very long time. For him, this wasn't romance or script. It was the only kind of love he understood: I can only touch when it's unbearable not to. Right now, I need you.

Lucien was still folded against her, shaking in uneven bursts. His hands clutched the fabric of her shirt like he feared gravity would rip him backward into the memories again. Yusra held him through it, arms firm around him, chin resting lightly on his hair. She breathed slowly, deliberately, so he would feel the rhythm and maybe anchor to it.

After a long silence, he whispered into her shoulder, voice thin as paper:

"After all of that... How can you still believe in God?"

Yusra tightened her arms around him, her cheek resting lightly against his hair. For a long moment, neither said anything.

Then, quietly:

"You know my favorite verse?" she whispered. "Three words. The whole Bible distilled into a heartbeat." She exhaled softly. "'God is love.'"

She let the words hover between them, gentle but unwavering.

"That verse is everything to me," she continued. "Not the weaponized passages. Not the purity codes. Not the politics. Just this: if God is love, then anything unloving is not God."

Lucien shivered, breathing unevenly.

"It's not just Christian for me," she went on, voice steadying into the scholar she was. "When I studied Islamic theology... the mystics, the philosophers, the Qur'anic commentaries... I found the same truth again and again."

She shifted slightly so she could see the side of his face.

"In Islam, life exists because God breathes life into it. Not symbolically. Literally. The divine breath animates creation."

Her voice warmed with conviction and wonder.

"That means anything alive is, in some way, carrying the divine within it. Not as gods. But as... extensions. Reflections. Expressions."

She brushed a strand of hair from his temple but didn't touch his skin.

"Christian mystics say the same thing," she murmured. "Christ in all things. Divinity shining through the world like sunlight through stained glass. Different colors, same light."

She swallowed, emotion tightening her throat.

"When I look at people, when I look at you, I don't see vessels waiting for salvation. I see fragments of the divine trying to survive a world hell-bent on forgetting its own sacredness."

He trembled.

"But you don't have to call it God," she whispered. "You don't even need to believe in divinity at all."

She placed her hand near his, close enough for him to feel her warmth.

"The point is: everything that lives has value because it lives. Because it breathes. Because it loves, or tries to."

Her voice softened even further.

"That is why 'God is love' matters to me. Because if God is love, then God is inside every living thing that knows love. Every act of compassion. Every choice toward truth."

She drew him closer, providing a solemn comfort into his chest.

"You don't need theology for that," she said gently. "You already live by it. Not because you believe in God. but because you believe in truth. Truth, Lucien... truth is the form love takes when it refuses to lie."

He let out a shaky breath, half sob, half relief. She held him tighter, as if she already knew this would be the last time she could. She held him like someone giving him back the one thing his world had taken from him:

Not God.
Not doctrine.
Not salvation.

A name for the thing he already lived for, and permission to define it in his own language. The storm outside had quieted into a low, steady hiss, rain soft against the windowpane, the kind of sound that usually soothed Lucien's nerves. Tonight, it only made the silence inside the apartment feel unnatural, like a held breath.

Yusra was still beside him on the couch, both of them leaning back now, breath finally evening out after the crash of memories and words. She hadn't moved far; their shoulders brushed every few seconds in a way that would've once sent him spiraling. Now it grounded him.

"You should sleep," she murmured. "You look like you've been awake for a week."

"I feel like I've been awake my entire life," he said.

She smiled tiredly. She rose to get him a glass of water, walking softly across the kitchen floor. Lucien's eyes followed her without meaning to. Something in his chest felt new, open, almost unbearably vulnerable. He didn't have language for it. He didn't need it.

The world was holding still.
Suspended.
Gentle.

Then—

A soft click.
Metal in the hallway.
A second click.
The kind that didn't belong to a front door.

Lucien's body snapped upright, every nerve in him screaming without knowing why.

"Yusra?" he whispered.

She turned from the sink at the same moment the apartment lights flickered. A thin, unnatural hum rippled through the air, low-frequency, deliberate, engineered. Her eyes widened. She recognized it.

"Lucien," she breathed, "get behind—"

The door exploded inward with black-clad, gloved hands, moving too quickly, too efficiently. No insignias. No warnings. Just the cold choreography of a state that had done this many times before. Yusra didn't scream. There was no time. One hand clamped over her mouth. Another seized her arms, wrenching them behind her so fast her glass shattered on the tile. Lucien froze, every instinct slamming against every trauma he had ever absorbed. His body refused to move. He hated it. He begged it. It refused.

"Wait—" he choked out, stumbling from the couch, "WAIT—she didn't—she's not—"

A baton struck his ribs. He collapsed, wind knocked out, panic cinching his lungs shut. He tried again to stand, reaching for her, but another blow cracked across his shoulder, sending his vision sparking white.

From the doorway, a muffled voice hissed, "Target secured. Extract now."

Yusra managed to twist her head toward Lucien, just enough for him to see her eyes. They held no fear for herself. Only urgency.

"Lucien," she tried to say around the hand covering her mouth. He read the shape of her lips.

Don't follow them.
Please.

He crawled toward her anyway. A boot stomped his hand. He screamed, a raw, animal sound. She struggled, eyes blazing, but the restraint was absolute. She couldn't reach him. She couldn't touch him. She couldn't speak. The last thing he saw was her being dragged backward into the dark hallway, rain streaking the open doorway behind her like vertical bars.

"YUSRA!"

His voice tore itself out of him, rough, unfamiliar, terrifying. The reply was the slam of the door. The sound of boots fading. The hum dying out. Then nothing. No warmth. No breath beside him. No presence in the room.

Just glass shards on the tile and the shape of her absence settling over him.

It didn't take long for the T-Regime to find him.

Lucien had collapsed onto the hard floor, shaking, Yusra's final surge of memories still flooding behind his eyes, the theology, the warmth of her arms around him, the monologue about God as love, the feeling of something true finally touching him. He'd never experienced anything like it. Then she had been taken.

He barely registered the boots pounding toward him before the needle went in. The room filled with a chalky, metallic gas. Some mysterious residue mixed with tranquilizer, and his already frayed mind caved instantly. His limbs dissolved into numbness.

The room swam out of focus. His thoughts scattered like glass. The last thing he remembered was the echo of her voice, telling him he was worthy of love.

Then—black.

He awoke upright, pulse hammering, wrists strapped to metal.

Visitation.

Cold restraints bit into his skin. The room was dim, lit only by a harsh white fluorescence that buzzed like an insect at his ear. His breath fogged lightly in the air. Ahead of him stood the one-way glass. Except this time, Crane wasn't facing the victim. He was facing him.

Black suit, black gloves, blank obsidian mask, the uniform of a Janaha in full ritual. The mask, though expressionless, felt almost aware as it fixed on Lucien. Lucien tried to speak, but the words caught in his throat. His selective mutism knotted hard, strangling any sound.

Crane tilted his head, as if savoring Lucien's silence.

"There is no quitting now, Dr. Tenebris," he said through the speaker system, calm, smooth, clinical. The voice of someone who felt nothing but the thrill of control. "Your segment and position are highly confidential... and critical to Vaughn's mission. Termination is not an option."

He stepped aside. The world dropped out of Lucien's chest.

Yusra hung from chained restraints bolted into the ceiling, her feet barely touching the ground. Her arms stretched above her head at a grotesque angle, wrists raw and bleeding around the shackles. Her body sagged, trembling, her blouse torn, skin marked with fresh welts.

Lucien inhaled sharply.

"YUSRA!"

His voice didn't make it through the glass. It was soundproof. The scream ripped his throat open anyway, raw and desperate. He strained against the restraints until metal scraped skin. His heartbeat roared. Every instinct in him fired: run, shield her, take her place, but he couldn't move.

Yusra didn't hear him. She felt him. Her eyes drifted to the glass, her own reflection staring back at her, bruised and wavering. Embedded inside it, faint, a blurred silhouette: Lucien's outline. His posture. His presence. She understood instantly. She swallowed, wincing, and whispered, lips trembling, voice thin.

"It's okay, Lucien. It's okay."

Her breath fogged just barely on the cold air in front of her. She forced her eyes open again, meeting her own reflection, speaking to the mirror because that was the only way she could reach him.

Crane paused at the sound. He turned. Slowly. His mask rotated toward her, then to the glass, then back to her again. His gloved hand twitched once at his side.

"What did you say?" he asked.

Yusra lifted her chin an inch, not out of defiance, but out of compassion. The kind he didn't understand.

"I said it's okay."

Crane's posture snapped. He crossed the room in three strides, the black mask filling her vision, and struck her across the face so hard the sound cracked through the entire chamber. Blood sprayed across the floor, a bright arc against the sterile concrete.

"Shut up," he growled.

Lucien tried to lunge, his whole body jerking forward, but the restraints held, metal rattling violently as he fought them. He was helpless. Yusra was being broken in front of him.

Blood dripped from Yusra's cheek in thin red rivulets, catching on the corner of her mouth. She spat a small strand onto the floor, breath shallow but steady. Crane stood over her, chest rising with quiet exhilaration.

Lucien watched helplessly, every muscle in his body pulled tight with panic.

Crane reached out. Two gloved fingers hooked beneath Yusra's chin and forced her face upward.

"Look at me," he whispered.

She didn't. She kept her eyes on her own reflection, and therefore, on Lucien. Crane's breath hitched, mirroring a predator irritated by divided attention.

"Fine," he said, lowering his hand, then grabbing the back of her neck, forcing his exposed thumb to brush the base of her skull below the hairline. For a moment, Lucien saw it again: that faint violet flicker sparking around Crane's thumb, the same color that had bloomed when he touched Yusra on the couch. But where Lucien had entered gently, Crane forced his way in like a knife.

The world flickered.

Crane inhaled as the connection snapped open, the Janaha entering her memories with invasive immediacy, a cold, plunging dive. Yusra's breath caught, her body arching against the chains. Lucien froze, watching the moment Crane invaded the most sacred parts of her mind. Behind the mask, Crane's pupils widened as memory after memory flooded him:

Yusra standing in the ruins of Gaza, soot in her hair, coughing smoke but clutching her research notes to her chest.

The war documentaries she studied frame-by-frame, hoping to understand suffering so she could help others understand God's love.

Her childhood church, stained glass refracting gold sunlight on her face.

Her mother praying in Arabic beside her, whispering ya Rabb, tears on her knuckles.

The day she arrived in America, hopeful, exhausted, defiant.

The moment she first heard Lucien's stuttered, awkward attempt at conversation.

The memory she shared with him only hours before:
"God is love. Every living thing is part of something divine."

Crane exhaled sharply. His hands trembled. His voice came out low, stunned, almost reverent:

"...oh."

Lucien's stomach twisted. Crane was enjoying it. Yusra squeezed her eyes shut, tears streaming down her face as Crane rifled through her life, her faith, her grief, her hope, chewing on them like a famished man.

"This..." Crane murmured, leaning closer, "...is exquisite."

He was high, but not satisfied. Not the way he got with a Bhuvaha, where the memories were not only felt, but projectable, transferable, extractable, perfect. He pulled his thumb away slowly, breathing harder, voice laced with frustrated hunger.

"Beautiful," he said. "But tragically... confined."

Yusra gasped at the release of his touch. Crane tilted his head, mask gleaming.

"You feel everything," he said quietly. "But you cannot give it to the world."

He stepped back, disappointed.

"No... this isn't enough."

He paced once across the room, his boots echoing.

"This will never be enough."

He turned back toward her, faster this time, his control cracked, the addict unmasked beneath the veneer of discipline. Lucien shook his head violently.

"Don't—"

No sound reached them. Crane reached for the metal baton on the table, fingers trembling with withdrawal.

"This," he said, voice soft and delighted, "is where we make our own memories."

Yusra's eyes met the mirror again. Her voice, barely a breath:

"It's okay, Lucien."

Crane circled her like a slow-moving fault line, each step adding pressure to the moment ticking toward rupture. Yusra hung from the restraints, breath ragged, her chest rising in shallow, trembling arcs. The baton in Crane's hand hummed faintly, not charged. Not yet. Just a promise.

Lucien had gone silent out of collapse. His throat clenched shut, his breath stuck halfway up his chest. His hands shook against the metal bindings, fingers twitching in broken stims that had nowhere to go.

Crane stopped beside her.

"Last chance," he murmured, though she'd been given none.

Yusra didn't lift her head. Didn't beg. Didn't scream. She just turned her face toward the mirror, toward Lucien's silhouette behind the glass, and breathed:

"My friend... you did not fail me."

Lucien's chest caved inward. A soft whimper escaped him, voiceless, just air.

Crane's posture tightened. Something in him recoiled at the softness between them, the kind of bond he could never taste, never extract, never own. He raised the baton. Slowly. Almost ceremonially.

The first strike landed across her ribs. Not enough to kill. Just enough to take the air out of her lungs. Yusra stifled her gasp; it came out as a choking, wet sound. Her knees buckled, chains jerking violently as her weight fell. Lucien jerked forward against the restraints so hard they cut into his wrists.

The second strike came faster. The third faster still. Each blow a crescendo building toward inevitability. Crane wasn't sloppy. He wasn't losing control. He was savoring. Yusra's breaths grew thinner, cracking around the edges. Her body was limp now, but the chains kept her upright, pulled taut like a puppet with snapped strings. Her head rested on her arm, eyes half-lidded. Still looking toward the mirror.

That was when Crane changed his grip. He switched from the baton to his gloved hands. Everything inside Lucien went cold.

Crane stepped behind her, placing one hand high on the chain above her wrists, steadying her weight. The other slid to the back of her head. Yusra didn't resist. Her breath fluttered once, like a candle in a draft. Crane leaned close, his mask nearly touching her hair.

"You should have been extraordinary," he said.

Then, without hesitation, he snapped her neck.

The sound was terrifyingly soft. A dry, muffled crack.
Barely more than a click. A sudden end so quiet it felt unreal.

Yusra's body slumped instantly, every muscle giving way at once. The chains caught her weight with a tiny metallic creak. Crane released the restraints. Her body dropped to the cold, hard floor, stolen of any chance to run.

Lucien's world froze. His throat clenched; no sound came. He wanted to run, to cradle her, to feel her steady breath one last time, but his limbs refused. Shock held him rigid, eyes locked on her lifeless form.

Gloved hands seized his arms. He barely resisted. The T-Regime guards dragged him through the sterile corridors, and then the glass-walled chamber loomed.

Inside, the walls were empty at first, then Alenya appeared, crisp in a cuffed military uniform, her gaze rising to meet his. Behind her, Secretary Drehl lingered, shadowed, whispering into her ear.

"It's time for your initiation, child," Drehl murmured. "You must press that button."

Alenya hesitated, voice trembling. "What will the button do to him?"

"It marks your official entrance into the T-Regime," Drehl replied, flat and unyielding.

Lucien watched, comprehension failing, as Alenya's gloved finger hovered over the switch. He muttered.

"Raven, please…"

When she pressed it, the air ignited.

Red smoke poured into the chamber, thick and acrid. It clawed at his lungs, stinging his eyes. Memories not his own, stolen, twisted, unbearable, flooded him. He convulsed, laughter ripping from him in between ragged sobs. His hands clawed at his skin, nails tearing into cheeks and forehead. Pain screamed through him, yet it barely registered over the storm of anguish inside his mind.

Bones felt like splintering wood, heart hammered against ribs as if trying to escape. Tears mingled with blood. Laughter spilled into a sound he no longer recognized as human.

Through the haze, he saw Alenya's face pressed against the glass, her gloved hand trembling as it struck the surface. His vision swam, darkness pooling at the edges, until it swallowed everything.

Outside, she fell to her knees. Blue blood spread beneath his prone form, vivid against the white floor. Alenya's whispered plea shattered the quiet:

"Father—something's wrong. He's not breathing right—this isn't normal—please, help him!"

Drehl's eyes were ice. "This is the fate of a Tapaha who cannot obey. Order demands obedience."

He turned and walked away, leaving Alenya crumpled, pressed

against the glass, staring at Lucien as if willing him to survive the unthinkable.

Lucien awoke on the cold tile of his Section 9 lab, lungs heaving, throat raw. Every breath felt like fire, the metallic tang of blood and the acrid smoke of Redline still clinging to him. Panic clawed at his chest.

He scrambled to his knees, hands shaking, and tore through drawers and counters, searching desperately. His eyes fell on a syringe.

"I… need this out," he rasped, fumbling to draw his own blood. The liquid that filled it gleamed blue, unnatural, shocking in its clarity. He stared, then a grin spread across his face, too wide, stretching his lips beyond reason.

"Hilarious," he whispered, then laughed. A brittle, ragged sound, fraying into full, manic cackling. He hummed along, a tune that didn't belong in the sterile room, rifling through drawers until he found a pair of latex gloves.

The door slammed open. A T-Regime guard filled the frame, vacant mask hiding intent.

"Tenebris. Report to your station," the voice said, calm and mechanical.

Lucien wiggled a finger, almost mockingly. "Tsk, tsk. No, no. No Lucien Tenebris here."

He grabbed a beaker, smashing it against the counter. Glass shards embedded in his gloved palm. Cold, precise, deliberate, he shoved the jagged edge into the guard's neck. The man gurgled, hands clutching uselessly at the wound, and crumpled to the floor.

Lucien stood over him, chest rising and falling in a manic rhythm, eyes wild and unblinking. His reflection in the glass of a nearby beaker stared back: blue-veined, chaotic, a thing reborn. Lucien Tenebris was the man who had loved truth and watched it be strangled. The man who'd begged and choked and frozen.

He lowered his head, listening to the new hum thrumming behind his eyes.

"Only... Paracelsus," he whispered, voice low, measured, dripping with something older than Lucien Tenebris. His laugh was gone, replaced by the quiet, inexorable certainty of someone who had survived the impossible and shed his former self like a skin.

The lab was still again, but he felt it: the lingering burn of the Redline, the echo of stolen memories, the faint coil of madness curling into a shape he could use. He was no longer a victim. He was an instrument. A mind unbound.

Somewhere, buried beneath the new circuitry, a part of him mourned, but that part was locked behind glass now, pressed to the window like a man watching his own body walk away under a different name.

XVI

They found him humming. The lab looked like a crime scene and a joke at the same time: glass glittering across the tile, a dead T-Regime officer bleeding out onto antiseptic white, a beaker still rolling in lazy circles near the body. Paracelsus stood at the center of it all, sleeves spattered with red and blue, head tilted as if listening to some music only he could hear.

Alarms howled in distant corridors, muffled by layers of reinforced concrete. Here, though, it was almost quiet. Just the buzz of the ventilation system, the soft drip of blood, the faint tremor of his own laughter still vibrating in his chest. He stepped neatly over the fallen guard and pranced into the hallway.

"Dr. Tenebris! Stand down!"

The shout ricocheted off the walls before the squad even turned the corner. Three white-suited officers, rifles leveled, boots pounding in coordinated rhythm. Paracelsus watched them approach as if they were an interesting specimen under glass.

"Dr. Tenebris," the lead repeated, breath slightly elevated beneath the voice modulator. "By order of Section Command, you are to surrender yourself for retrieval and reconditioning. Kneel and place your hands on your head."

Paracelsus smiled.

"Oh no," he said pleasantly. "Lucien Tenebris surrendered himself hours ago. You're quite late."

He lifted his hand. It still bled sluggishly inside the latex glove where the shards had embedded. A single trembling piece of glass caught the corridor light. The first officer hesitated. The flicker was all Paracelsus needed. He moved.

It wasn't graceful, not really. It was too fast, too jagged, more like a misfired reflex than calculated strategy, yet somehow worked. He crashed into the lead officer, shoulder driving into sternum, the beaker shard punching up under the man's chin. Warmth spilled over his glove. The officer dropped, rifle clattering. He giggled, watching the officer's body crash to the ground.

The second fired on instinct.

Rounds tore into the wall and ceiling. One caught Paracelsus along the ribs; he laughed, breath hitching, pivoted with the impact, and slammed the dead officer's body into the shooter. They went down in a heap of white and red.

"Stop him! Sedation protocol—now!"

The third officer had already dropped to one knee, sighting along the barrel of a sleek, silver rifle. Not standard issue. A slender vial clipped beneath the chamber pulsed with faint red, the liquid inside glowing like a captured ember. Paracelsus saw it and went still, eyes brightening with recognition.

"Oh," he breathed. "Looks like the T-Regime got some new toys!"

The dart hit him in the side of the neck. He staggered, hand flying up too late. The world lurched in on itself. The corridor stretched, contracted, then blurred at the edges like bad film stock. Redline sang in his veins, waking up the ghosts of every memory he'd ever touched, every horror he'd ever folded into himself. The tranquilizer rode in on its back like a quiet, patient rider. His knees hit the floor. He laughed once, high and sharp, even as his limbs turned to wet sand.

"Clever," he slurred. "Chemical... diplomacy..."

The hallway folded into itself and went dark.

Secretary Drehl and Alenya stood on the other side of the glass prison door, watching Paracelsus's slumber. Alenya's gloves were still on.

She stood smaller than she felt, spine held rigid by sheer will and conditioning, white uniform pressed and cuffed, boots aligned perfectly with the seam in the floor. Her gloved hands were clasped behind her back, mirroring the posture of the man beside her without realizing she'd copied it.

Secretary Drehl didn't need the uniform to command the room. The black suit, the simple tie, the small pin at his lapel bearing Vaughn's crest were enough. His gaze rested not on Paracelsus at first, but on Alenya.

"You understand what this is," he said quietly.

Alenya swallowed. Her voice came out softer than she wanted.

"He's... compromised," she managed. "Tapaha subjected to uncontrolled Redline exposure are... unpredictable liabilities to the regime. Standard protocol is extermination."

"Correct," Drehl said. He let the word hang a beat, then added, "For most."

He turned his eyes toward the glass. On the other side, Paracelsus had rolled onto his side, tucking his hands under his cheek as he slumbered.

"Dr. Lucien Tenebris," Drehl went on, voice clinical. "Brilliant, fragile, inconveniently moral."

Alenya's jaw tightened at the 'was' he didn't say aloud.

"What we have now," Drehl continued, "is something different."

He looked back at her.

"What do we call a Tapaha who has survived saturation, whose mind has broken and reformed around Redline instead of drowning in it?"

Alenya's brow furrowed. She searched for a term in the carefully sanitized files she'd been allowed to read. There wasn't one.

"I don't know, Father," she admitted.

Drehl's mouth curved a fraction. Not quite a smile.

"We call him useful," he said. "We call him Paracelsus."

Alenya's eyes flicked to the man on the floor.

"Paracelsus," she repeated, testing the shape of it.

"He is no longer Lucien Tenebris," Drehl said. "Lucien was sentimental. Lucien wanted to quit." His gaze sharpened. "Paracelsus will not."

Drehl stepped closer to Alenya. Not touching. Close enough that she could feel the heat of his attention.

"You asked once," he said, "why we work so diligently to find children like you. Do you remember?"

Alenya kept her eyes forward. "Yes, Father."

"It is because the state requires shepherds," Drehl said. "Guides for those too valuable to discard, too dangerous to trust." He inclined his head toward the cell. "Paracelsus is one such creature. He is brilliant. Devastated. Malformed by what he has seen. Left alone, he will destroy himself and our work with him. Shaped correctly, he will change the world."

He let that settle, then:

"He is yours now."

Alenya's breath caught. "Mine?"

"Your pet. Your project. Your responsibility," Drehl said. "You will learn from him. You will direct him. You will ensure his genius serves order, not chaos."

Her fingers twitched inside her gloves.

"How?" she asked, before she could stop herself.

Drehl's eyes softened by half a degree. Approval, in his way.

"Take off your right glove," he said.

The room felt suddenly smaller.

Alenya's gaze snapped to his bare hand, then to her own.

"But—Father, you said recruits are never to be ungloved in secure sectors without explicit—"

"This is explicit," he cut in, gentle but absolute. "You are no ordinary recruit. You are Tapaha. So is he. You will not shatter each other. You will simply see."

Her throat worked. Slowly, fingers trembling, she peeled the glove from her right hand. The air felt raw against her skin, too bright, too loud. Every nerve along her palm woke up at once.

Drehl nodded toward a small panel beside the glass. "Door."

The air-sealed door hissed open.

Paracelsus, still Lucien in body, though the name no longer fit, lay unconscious on the cold tile floor. His breathing was shallow, his limbs slack, his face streaked with dried blood and chemical residue from the tranquilizer and Redline exposure. He did not stir when Alenya approached. Her boots stopped just inches from his curled form.

He looked small like this. Fragile, even. Not at all like the man who had run through corridors, killed officers, screamed himself raw in the gas chamber. He looked... empty. Not peaceful. Alenya swallowed, the bare skin of her right hand trembling in the cold air. Drehl's voice came through the intercom, soft as a knife sliding between ribs:

"Wake him, child."

Her throat tightened. "Father... how?"

"With your gift," Drehl said. "Tapaha to Tapaha. You will see who he is now."

She knelt beside the unconscious man. His face twitched in some unremembered nightmare, lips parting with the ghost of a gasp. His body was here, but the self behind it flickered like a dying bulb.

Alenya reached out. Her bare palm hovered above his forearm. Just touching him felt like pressing her hand toward a storm. She closed her eyes, whispering, "I'm sorry," not sure why she said it, then lowered her hand. Her skin met his.

The world exploded.

A violet shock ripped through the cell, not light, not sound, but impact. Like two tectonic plates slamming together. Lucien's body arched upward, spine bowing off the floor, breath tearing into his lungs as if he had been drowning inside himself. His eyes shot open. They were not Lucien's eyes.

They were wide, bright, glassy with newborn clarity, like someone seeing the world for the very first time.

At the same moment, Alenya felt the rupture:

A chunk of memory. A corridor of thoughts. A cluster of identity tore itself out of him. Not a moment. Not an event. A self.

For a split second she saw the fragments leaving him:

The two officers he killed.
The lab floor slick with blood.
The elevator button.
The gas chamber.
Yusra's body dropping
The last scream
The last breath
The last piece of Lucien
"I quit."

Then—

Nothing. A hollow. A perfect absence. Lucien Tenebris didn't drift away. He ceased.

Alenya's palm ripped from his skin, but it was too late. The wipe had carved out the entire topography of who he had been. His body collapsed back to the tile, breathing hard, stunned like a newborn creature.

Then, slowly, he lifted his head. His gaze found her immediately, locking onto her with eerie precision. His restraints clinked as he shifted, as if testing the weight of a body he had never worn before. He whispered, voice raw, completely untethered from Lucien's memories:

"...Raven?"

She froze. Behind the glass, Drehl inhaled, delighted. Paracelsus struggled to sit up, wrists bound, but eyes sharp with curiosity, not confusion.

"What... happened?" he asked softly. "Was I... asleep?"

He blinked slowly, focusing on her bare hand.

"No..." he whispered to himself. "It's more than that. Something ended."

His head tipped, as if listening to a voice only he could hear.

"He is gone," he said simply.

Not mournful. Not confused. Certain. He lifted his gaze fully to Alenya, studying her with unsettling clarity.

"And I am awake."

A smile crept across his mouth, slow, dawning, warm and wrong all at once.

"Tell me what I am, Raven."

Alenya's breath hitched. Drehl's voice filled the cell from above, smooth and triumphant:

"You are Paracelsus."

Paracelsus looked at the ceiling, then back at Alenya.

"Paracelsus," he repeated, as if tasting the sound.

He nodded once, satisfied.

"That is mine."

He leaned closer, bound hands shifting toward her.

"And you," he murmured, soft with impossible trust, "are the first face I have ever seen."

Alenya swallowed hard. She had awakened him. She had erased Lucien. She had birthed something new.

Paracelsus, bright-eyed, reborn, terrifyingly lucid, whispered.

"Don't leave me in suspense, Raven. What mischief are we about to get into?"

XVII

The mirror reflected a man carved out of cold intention.

Vaughn adjusted the platinum pin at his lapel, a sigil no one else yet understood, not truly. They thought it a commemorative emblem, something minted for tonight's ceremony. They did not know it was older than the republic, older than his presidency, older even than the language stamped on their currency. They did not know it belonged to a ritual buried in the shadows of the Janaha, a ritual he had resurrected and renamed with clinical elegance.

The Ministry of the Vale.

Outside the antechamber, applause rose in disciplined waves, echoing through the marble corridors like a tidal heartbeat. His administration believed tonight was about unveiling the *Enclaves*, forty-two months of structural reform culminating in a neatly packaged geopolitical triumph.

Let them believe it. The map would be the distraction. The Vale would be the truth.

A gentle knock.

"Mr. President," his advisor called, voice tight with awe. "It's time."

Vaughn didn't move at first. He let his gaze linger on the mirror a moment longer. The sigil glinted with the faintest violet sheen under the lights, a color traditionally forbidden in the government chambers, but no one questioned him anymore. He had earned that obedience.

He murmured, barely audible, "Thirteen cycles. As it should be."

The number threaded through every stage of his rise: thirteen security amendments repealed, thirteen "restructurings," thirteen purges framed as civic uplift. Now the thirteenth night of the winter cycle, the night the Vale would step from shadow into circuitry, masked beneath the language of national rebirth.

He stepped forward.

The attendant opened the door, and the sound crashed into him like surf: cheers, the tremor of cameras, the mechanical pulse of stage lights. Underneath, faint, nearly imperceptible, Vaughn heard the other rhythm. The one he had built in the underground chambers sealed beneath the Rotunda. The one only the highest circle of Janaha and elite officials would recognize when the hour grew late and the guards were dismissed.

A hum. A chant. A promise. Suffering distilled. Trauma consecrated.

The captive Bhuvaha would be brought in after the ceremony, blindfolded, trembling, drugged to the threshold of their gift. Their memories would bloom raw in the dark, exposed nerve after exposed nerve. That exquisite breaking, the agony that fed the ritual, would sanctify the Vale for another cycle.

He imagined the chamber now: candles trembling in recessed alcoves, stone masks awaiting their bearers, the ceremonial bowl placed at the center like an awaiting mouth. He had refined the practices, organized them, given them a modern, clinical clarity. No more folktale murk. No superstition. A system. A sacrament.

Through torment, truth.
Through truth, obedience.
Through obedience, order.

When he stepped onto the stage, the Rotunda erupted. Flags unfurled. Confetti cannons burst. Children with rehearsed smiles waved at him from their designated row. Everything looked celebratory, patriotic, almost holy. Perfect camouflage.

He touched the podium, feeling the cool metal under his palm. His speech lay in front of him, a scripted proclamation of unity and rebirth. The real birth was happening beneath their feet.

"The Enclaves," he began, voice steady and magnified through the hall, "mark a new era."

Applause swallowed the words. He waited, smiling like a man promising light rather than manufacturing darkness.

"...an era where safety is sanctified. Where order is restored. Where truth is no longer a matter of interpretation, but of devotion."

The cameras flashed. Only the chosen few felt the meaning beneath the phrasing. Only the chosen knew what waited at cycle's end tonight.

As he concluded, the crowd rose to its feet in worship, and Vaughn lifted his chin, accepting the adoration like a benediction. History would remember this night as the founding of a cleaner nation, a safer nation.

He knew better. This was the Thirteenth Night. The birth of the Enclaves.

Deep beneath the marble and gold, behind sealed stone doors and ritual masks, the Ministry of the Vale inhaled its first full breath.

Author's Notes

Genesis began as a question I couldn't shake:

How does someone become entangled in harm while still believing themselves to be good? How do we unlearn the stories that shaped us?

Where *[UNTITLED.]* came from the scar, *Genesis* comes from the wound. It traces not only the birth of a dystopian world, but the quiet, complicated making of a man who will one day be remembered as both a caution and a catalyst. Lucien Tenebris was never a villain to me. He was the part of myself I spent years trying to understand, the part that masks, that performs, that learns rules by studying everyone else, that wants desperately to do the right thing but has been taught to fear the wrong threats.

Lucien's autism is deeply personal to me. I grew up undiagnosed for nearly thirty years, moving through the world as someone who felt everything intensely but often struggled to decode the social worlds around me. I understood emotion through pattern, logic, and repetition. I understood connection through attentiveness and sincerity. It took me a long time to realize there was nothing wrong with that, that my brain wasn't broken; it was simply wired for a different kind of understanding.

Writing Lucien allowed me to honor the parts of my neurodivergence I once tried to hide. His stims, his need for order, his sensory overwhelm, his nonlinear processing: these are pieces of me. They were not added for representation; they were written because they are my daily reality.

Lucien's asexuality echoes another quiet truth in my life. I am demisexual, and for many years I didn't have language for why intimacy did not look or feel the way people told me it should. Lucien's orientation is not a plot device; it is a window into the gentler rhythms of desire, trust, and emotional connection that resonate with me personally. His way of loving is slow, cautious, and deeply intentional, a mirror I didn't realize I needed.

Yusra's voice, on the other hand, carries a different part of me. Her philosophical grounding, her willingness to challenge institutions, her insistence on thinking beyond the narratives handed to her, all of these grew out of my own journey of unlearning and deconstruction. Like her, I questioned the traditions I was raised in. I asked what morality becomes when authority distorts it. I learned to sit with contradictions, to trace systems back to their roots, to refuse the simplifications that make cruelty feel orderly.

If Lucien is the part of me that searches for belonging, Yusra is the part of me that refuses to let comfort become complicity.

Together, they let me tell the story I never knew how to speak aloud: that indoctrination is quiet, that harm can come wrapped in purpose, and that the way out is anchored in connection, curiosity, and self-recognition.

Genesis is about the making of a dystopia, yes, but it is also about the making of a human being inside a system that rewards obedience over empathy. It is about the thin line between survival and surrender, and about the courage it takes to step away from a story you were told was the only one available.

If this book resonates with you, I hope it reminds you that unlearning is possible at any age, and that there is no shame in growing differently than you were expected to. Every fracture inside us can become an opening. Every truth we claim can become a beginning.

Beginnings, even the painful ones, are their own kind of genesis.

This story also marks the moment the world within these novels begins to strip away the very traits that make us human, our sensitivities, our neurodivergence, our queerness, our philosophical curiosity, our capacity for deep feeling. It is the origin point of a system built on the idea that difference is dangerous, that divergence must be corrected, and that beauty exists only in sameness. In that sense, *Genesis* reflects how ableism takes root: quietly, methodically, through the insistence that certain bodies, minds, and ways of being must be hidden, disciplined, or erased to preserve an illusion of "order."

Writing this book helped me confront how often our own world tries to sand down those same parts of us, the traits that make us vivid, complex, and irreplaceably alive.

If *Genesis* shows the birth of a system determined to eliminate those qualities, then I hope it also shows the quiet, stubborn truth that no system can extinguish what makes us beautifully human.

www.ingramcontent.com/pod-product-compliance
Lightning Source LLC
Chambersburg PA
CBHW061424160726

47995CB00003B/747